THE COURAGE TO BE MARRIED

The Courage to Be Married

By
JONATHAN HANAGHAN

With a Preface by
LUDOVIC KENNEDY

COMPILED AND EDITED BY
BRENDAN McGANN

A PRIORITY EDITION

ABBEY PRESS
St. Meinrad, Indiana 47577

1976

First Published in U.S.A., 1974
Second Printing, July 1975
Third Printing, October 1975
Fourth Printing, January 1976
Fifth Printing, February 1976

Library of Congress Catalog Card Number: 73-94166
ISBN 0-87029-020-7

CONTENTS

EDITOR'S NOTE

The book was compiled from a series of discussions given by Jonathan Hanaghan which were tape-recorded. Because the printed page, unlike the spoken word, allows everyone to peruse things at his own pace, my problem was to remove what the linguists call the 'redundancy' of the spoken word without disrupting the essential fluency of Jonty's ideas. It has not been possible to do this at all times but I decided to allow any repetition in the book to remain rather than do further violence to the poetry and dynamics of Jonty's vision of life. I wish to thank Rupert Strong for giving me the opportunity to edit the book.

BRENDAN McGANN

August 1973

ACKNOWLEDGEMENTS

Acknowledgement is due to the help of Maurice Henry, Dr. J. Fanibunda, and Dr. M. Hartman, who arranged and edited the first manuscript which was the basis on which the Editor, Brendan McGann, worked.

PREFACE

Very occasionally in life one meets people who make a great impact on one, people who stand out from the common run, *extra*-ordinary beings. For me Jonty Hanaghan was one. I first met him in Belfast when we were both taking part in the programme on Ulster Television, and I was struck, as so many others had been before me, not only by his magnificent physical presence, the lion head and mane of white hair, but also by a curious blend of what seemed at some moments like saintliness and at others like exhibitionism. He radiated some quality which was quite primitive and fundamental, something, I imagine, that Christ his master and all great healers have always possessed; a sense of inner peace, of calm after storm, of concord and conciliation, of journey's end. His spirit talked to the unawakened spirits of others; and it was this, as he well knew himself, that drew people of all types towards him to be touched and healed.

I cannot pretend to be much of an authority on books about marriage, but if there is another that goes more directly to the heart of the matter, that tells us more bluntly and beautifully what marriage is and is not about, I have yet to read it. The words leap from the page as spontaneously and warmly as they once leapt from his lips. These pages, so skilfully and unobtrusively edited, convey the essence of the man, his concern for humankind, his courage and compassion. Listen to this.

'... the tragedy of our age is that we are packed with sexual knowledge and are bankrupt of sexual understanding.'

'As you know, the majority of psycho-analysts have no interest in religion. They are so fascinated with their own science that they don't press beyond it. I press beyond it...'

'You can be sure of one thing—that however beautiful a woman is, she is a bitch, and if you have never found that out, you have never found a woman.'

'If you try to compel your wife or your husband not to be like themselves but to be like you or someone you like, you are offending against human relations and human personality.'

'... the central factor in the analyst's healing is the analyst's capacity to love. And by love I mean the spiritual capacity to give another person utter freedom of heart to say and to feel what they like without condemnation.'

'Civilisation has been built on the sublimation of the sexual impulse.'

'Men with their imagination are easily attracted by beauty ... they're easily allured. But I assure you that is on the surface only. Men are not fools, when trouble comes, when things go wrong, they come every time to the fundamental woman. That is why it is foolish to worry when their eyes wander....'

And then this, which is really the core of it all.

'... marriage isn't worth a hell, it isn't worth a penny, until one or the other has the courage to strike into the fundamental narcissism of the other, and lay it bare, and fight any spiritual fight that is necessary to bring one's mate to reality with oneself.... When she can bring all her hate on to me, and say all she feels about me, then I know I've touched the ultimate narcissism in this woman. I've touched the ultimate agony in her. I've touched the things that have wounded her most, and she is finding her release by destroying me. And this is my necessity; to accept the danger of the destruction, to accept the cross, as the ancient Christians would say, not to abandon the woman.'

'Such a courageous, such an essential attitude will blow your marriage sky-high if it's not rooted in love. If it turns out that it's not rooted in love, and you are to disturb this growling beast down in the fundamental depth of the unconscious, wilder than any wild beast, you'll be destroyed by it. Or you will discover that she is not your woman, or he is not your man ... That brave acceptance

of the danger of marriage, this crisis of marriage, is the
reality of love.'

That is a fundamental truth about marriage. But how
many married couples know about it, and of those how
many have availed themselves of it? Let us hope that
after this book is published there will be more.

I saw Jonty only once more after our meeting on a series of religious programmes in which interviewers were
invited to talk to people who had impressed them, but who
were unknown to the general public. I chose Jonty. In
ten years of working for television, I cannot recall any
interview which has given me greater satisfaction. Too
often in television interviews, one is trying to prise away
the defensive masks that so many put up, trying to discover what really is in their hearts. With Jonty one had
no need for this. He gave what was in his heart, freely
and fully; and I believe there were many that night who,
after listening to what he said, were made a little more
aware of the fullness and diversity of life, and of their
own capacity to enjoy it.

I count it a great privilege to have met this man, even
if briefly, and to have benefited, as so many did, from the
rich store of his being. And for those that didn't have
that privilege, I hope that these pages, in which his voice
rings out so truly, will do something of the same.

LUDOVIC KENNEDY

May 1973

SUITS
OF
ARMOUR

CHAPTER ONE

I doubt if five per cent of married people in Europe to-day have a real, rich, natural, spiritual, sexual relationship. I doubt if five per cent of the marriages today in any way encompass the passion that the Creator intended or the beauty that He intended when He made the magnificent creatures of his, man and woman.

In my opinion, it takes ten years to make a genuine, fundamental, well-knit, true marriage, ten years in which you are learning patience with each other, ten years in which you are learning understanding of each other's different outlook, and above all in which you are trying to understand the profound mystery of sexual difference —for sexual difference is a profound mystery. We think it isn't because with our biological cleverness we analyse the physical side of sex and with our psychological cleverness we lay bare the intellectual side of marriage. But transcending these is the spiritual aspect of the relationship. Until man and woman have carried their confrontation to the point where they discover the real essence of each other, they have not learned the real meaning of the sex relationship: they have not come face to face with the mystery of it all. Because the end of it all is mystery. Until they reach the point where, like the Greeks, they are filled with wonder, they have not discovered the real beauty of a fulfilled sexual relationship.

Youth is now exploring this intangible world of spiritual loveliness where a man does not know his manhood until it is mirrored and presented in womanhood, and a woman does not know her womanhood until it is presented in the spirituality of a man who loves her.

Youth is seeking, innocently and profoundly and deeply and sincerely, for the exploration not of the external space of the physical world but the interior spaces of the sexual soul of man and woman.

The young sense the hypocrisy of our respectability, the futility of our suits of armour designed to secure us from the risks of emotional mobility. The poets, especially the English poets, have always sensed the beauty and graciousness of the true sexual life. Spenser gives us the vision of a boy looking into a girl's eyes, seeing the beauty that she herself does not know; he tells her of the beauty that is in her soul, and she can't see it, but through his words and his glances, she awakes to him and her soul is born into immortal beauty. She responds to him and is literally made, re-created by his love, for the lover literally creates his beloved; she becomes something that she never imagined she could have been.

Women for centuries have been raped and destroyed by the inability of men and women to sense the beauty and the holiness that is the sexual life, and their bodies have simply been the receptors of masturbatic satisfaction for their men and nothing more. And they have become bitter. The women's movement that occurred prior to the First World War was the first rebellion. When these women leaped to the call of votes for women, they weren't interested really in votes for women: they were interested in something so deep and so profound and so unknown that they could only state it in this crude way, in crying out for votes.

For we have hurt the whole ethos of life by the things that we have accepted in our cynicism. But the youth of today are not accepting them. And we are either beholding an absolute, major breakdown in sexuality which will destroy our culture or we are beholding a new seeking, a new searching, a new sensing of values, a new ache for an unknown land. And youth themselves can't tell you anything about it because they are only beginning the adventure. It's ridiculous to get them to talk about it because they are often dumb with the beauty of it, perplexed by the discovery of this immense hidden dimension of life. This adventure is far more serious than the adventure into time-space, far more important than the spectacular journeys to the moon, for this is nothing less than youth entering into a new interior dimension, a dimension in my opinion utterly necessary if people are to even begin to know the meaning of the kingdom of heaven that is within everyone.

I don't think our traditional form of Christianity can touch this; our dilemma is that we belong to an older generation. We would have to take the shoes from off our feet before entering because the ground is holy. But even more difficult, we would have to leave behind our suits of armour, our conventions, and become truly honest again, become 'as little children.'

Youth are even daring to ask if our present marriage systems and our arrangements of society are correct? Have we made many mistakes? Have we put holiness onto perishable things, have we demanded that which is only tenable at a certain period of time, have we made it into an eternal command? Are we demanding that the soul be chained unto orders enunciated centuries ago which might have been adequate to the insight of man at that time but is no longer adequate to the deeper, profounder, more tender understanding of the relationship of man to woman? This is the problem, and youth is on the adventure. Youth make many mistakes but they are out to seek a new age, and I think it is up to the grown-up people to admit to youth: 'You are ahead of us. We were caught in a maelstrom of stupidity and war; we can only point to all the shattered, dead bodies of all the youth of all the world: that's all we did for our generation while we pretended love, we pretended the kingdom of God.' The elders of the world sent out their youth to protect the fatherland

and all they did was protect the fathers. The fatherlands perished but, by God, the fathers didn't! They lasted on while youth killed youth for the fathers. And the killing hasn't stopped!

I therefore regret any harsh attitude taken against youth even if youth does an apparent wrong. I am against youth being squashed if they write something that elders think shocking. I hold that we should have the courage to know. We're not going to be wounded by words. We're only going to be wounded by lack of intellectual integrity and we should not be afraid of freedom, of giving all people their freedom, believing that in the end they will find thereby the light.

We all have to learn; and we can't learn while we're talking, only while listening. But are we really listening to our youth? For when we break out in bloody war, we are only committing mass murder to explode the imponderable, immense gathering of murder and hate in our hearts that has to find a way out in the end. Our great mass wars are not the product of diplomacy and they are not the product of economic conflictions, as the economists say, for you can't have war without a dynamic; you can't produce war without men wanting to murder people, and no man wants to murder anyone unless he is a murderer in his heart. No soldier could be compelled to murder anyone if he has not latent murder in his soul.

'What has all this got to do with marriage?' you may ask. Marriage is the foundation-stone of our society and I think that there can be very little argument that the type of society we have must reflect the type of marriages in that society. Most children grow up in the bosom of their families and nothing affects them as much as the atmosphere in the home in which they were reared. There are many signs however that give the lie to the respectable front presented by most marriages. Behind the curtains there is sedition and sometimes not just behind the curtains. What are some of these signs?

Take the case of a girl who has been apparently a perfect and beautiful wife. But at a certain stage she begins to read a lot of novels, particularly romantic novels. At her bedside you will see book after book of this type. Some people may smile and regard this as a harmless diversion. But the tragedy is that for some reason she has turned away from her husband and is living in a world of fantasy, the world of easy stories. These stories are not written by great artists who take you through the agony and the sweat and the tears as the great novelists do. Rather they are badly written and shoddy, always producing endings which gratify. The wife's behaviour indicates the absence of a full, rich marriage. It is a marriage which in fact is breaking; and the cleavage is so subtle that the average man or wife won't spot this type of warning signal. The man for his part sometimes finds interest in an absorbing hobby, giving all sorts of excuses why his hobby must have so much time spent on it. But the wife will soon see that the hobby is in fact his first love. The original unity, the passionate joy, the acclaim that used to be between the lovers has gone.

On the other hand, what about the married men who go to the pub and drink night after night, having endless foolish conversations with their own sex and spending money which should be used for the maintenance of their wives and children? These men are in fact finding a lot of their emotional life with their fellows. They become imbued with a false type of masculinity which considers being with men more masculine than being with their wives. But the only real type of masculinity is the type that can survive and live with man's proper mate, woman. For in the marriage arena, your pretences are laid bare. The real challenge of two completely different people living together must be met face to face. And when a man finds that his beautiful, pliant little wife has got a will of iron or when the wife finds that her hero, for whom she has just made a beautiful meal, wants to slip off to the pub for a couple of drinks, reality dawns. And this sort of thing can either be faced and understood or it can be side-tracked by pretence and delusion, by donning a suit of armour and by maintaining appearances above all. So the husband resorts to spending most of his time with 'the lads' and the wife repairs to her novelettes.

Of course there are many other manifestations of their unwillingness in marriage to face the real crunch of living together. A wife, for example, may allow her love to come back on herself, to envelop herself in the love which should be going out to her husband. She may become very interested in her dresses and her make-up and her toilet; she may become herself a full-time project for herself. Other signs of the reluctance of the partners to come to grips in a marriage are the twin problems of birth-control and over-large families. Here is an example of the way in which so-called 'modern' people have a surfeit of knowledge of sex but very little real understanding of it. It is a terrible thing for a Catholic woman to have to be loyal to the teaching of her Church on the one hand, but on the other hand to be faced with the likelihood of successive unwanted pregnancies. Woman suffers few burdens worse than that of the unwanted child, the child who is borne in desolation and loneliness. Man's education is so barren in this respect that most men are quite unaware of the spiritual disturbance that is in a woman when she is with child if the child is not the utterance of significance between herself and her husband. If the baby is not born of the spirit of a love-expression between the couple but is just the result of sex-hunger, then the woman is anguished and alone with her burden.

It is not much different with husbands and wives who, when having sex relations, withdraw so as to prevent conception. They rationalise it by saying they can't afford another child; there is the car to run and the house to be paid for and after all they must keep up a certain standard of living. But as the days go by and the woman is barren, there is a cry in her heart, a longing for a child. But she doesn't realise the real problem because she has committed herself to a philosophy which runs counter to her nature.

I once treated a woman who was in a desperate state of sickness, well nigh unto complete mental breakdown. Her husband was a brilliant and well-known clergyman. However, they not only slept in separate beds but in separate bedrooms; and when the desire came over one or the other of them, they made love, but they had no love, and she confessed to me that even if he made love to her, she imagined that she was in a boat going up the river in Cambridge when she was a student and had had a lover, and she imagined the other man was her lover as her husband was making love to her in order to get some feeling of sexual excitement. This is a shattering type of situation, not uncommon, which however tends to happen to women more often than men. Once they have their gratification, many men lack the sensitivity to know that their mate is unsatisfied. They fail to see the significance of it at a time like that when, for example, the woman simply sighs and turns on her side. The woman is not expressing her unhappiness verbally, but is expressing it nonetheless. And often men are too immersed in their own sensual satisfaction to notice.

Any number of men today think that the sexual act is a physical copulation following impulsive desire. They don't regard it as a shy and delicate approach to another spirit, a delicate and beautiful seeking out of interior loveliness of heart and mind. It is not to them some adventure akin to art and literature, some adventure into this mysterious land of femininity, the art of wooing. And the women, for their part, respond with an indifference to sensuality, a reluctance to indulge in the frank physical abandonment which alone is the true pleasure and one of a well-balanced marriage. The result is a very prevalent sexual starvation. No woman says: 'I hunger for real sex more than I hunger for bread.' Women are often too false to their own selves to admit that. And the reason is that they doubt the answering capacities of their mates. A woman would rather delude herself in this way when she fears that her man would not understand her ache, her unfulfilment. You very rarely encounter a home where there is an obvious, radiant, sexual fulfilment. But when there is such fulfilment, the atmosphere in the home reflects it. The husband and wife are very obviously a pair.

But for a couple who fail to forge themselves into a pair, the split in the home soon becomes obvious. And some of the deepest disillusions in a marriage occur at the point of coitus. After making love, instead of contentment, there is a wistfulness, a sadness, a loneliness, and each goes to sleep troubled and separate.

Sooner or later, people who are psycho-sexually starved in this way find diversions which destroy the marriage further. A woman tells the secrets of her marriage to her friend who you may be quite sure passes the word on. The man may express his dissatisfaction with the marriage state in general to his mates who, because they may be in similar situations, will understand him perfectly. Sooner or later, the wife in getting advice from her friend's husband, finds that her body responds rapturously to another man's in a way it never did to her husband's. She is faced with the amazing truth that the capacity for orgastic feelings wells up more in an apparently accidental friendship like that than with her own husband. In the same way, when a man gets some caress or consolation from a sympathetic girl, all the pent-up yearnings that are in him are allowed expression. So there begins an immense network of secret relationships. And following on these come the rationalisations to justify it all; and the most popular of these is the doctrine of free love. Such people often develop a model theory of freedom of sex. And they often end up believing that they are fighting for the survival of such freedom whereas in fact all they are fighting for is the continuance of their own distorted behaviour. And the tragic thing is that according to American statistics, for example, seventy-five per cent of those who go on this sex 'freedom' binge return in the end to try and renew the original relationship which they never really consummated in the first place.

I know this all sounds very tragic and difficult; on this basis the marriage relationship would seem to be, if not a hopeless adventure, at least a terribly difficult one. But I hope to show in the remainder of this book that through the insights of psycho-analysis, we can learn the origin of many of these failures and thus prevent them from occurring, if we are prepared to fight the battle of the sexes.

DE
PROFUNDIS

CHAPTER TWO

Now if everyone who got married were fully matured and had had a normal upbringing, there would be no problem, no need for this book. But we all know this is not the case. In this chapter I want to show you how the techniques used in psycho-analysis can be used just as effectively by the partners to a marriage if they have some insight into the situation and if they are prepared to make the effort, the effort of love. The closeness of the marriage relationship forces people to unmask their pretences and in doing this there is a great opportunity for personal growth. Wives can be quite sure that if their husbands are prepared to argue and fight with them, they really care; they are being honest enough to come out into the open with it. And husbands should be thankful if their wives come straight out and tell them what they think of them. This is a very healthy situation and I will show you later on why this is so.

If, however, you prefer to remain a hypocrite and hold back your real feelings, if you decide to put on a 'suit of armour,' of respectability, then your marriage can never be more than a sham. You may even bolster up your hypocrisy with religion and present an appearance of holy patience: 'Oh, yes, my husband is a wonderful man. Of

course, now and again, he's a little difficult but then we
are all difficult, aren't we?' But sooner or later, this sort
of mythological Christian marriage which has been laud-
ed to high heaven as the ultimate value of life, where one
never quarrels, but lives happily ever after, sooner or
later cracks wide open and all the hypocrisy is laid bare
for all to see. Such Sunday-school marriages are weak and
futile; they produce nothing worthwhile. And such hypocrisy can go on for years where the husband and wife
do not have the courage to face the issues and battle them
out. But fulfilment was intended by the Creator; marriage was not meant to be an economic arrangement but
a source of personal growth for both partners. But growth
involves honesty and change and pain; and I will tell
you why. If you are going to fuse two metals together
you can only fuse them when the white heat is such that
the metals begin to melt; only then can you fuse the two
metals together so that they become one. In a similar
way, until all the qualities, high and low, belonging to a
man and a woman—the hate, the love, the anger, the contempt, the sneering—until all these are accessible to the
marriage experience, you cannot get the frank situation
in which there can be a fusion of hearts and minds and
spirits. You don't get the atmosphere and you can't get
the intensity whereby two people may become one. You
can only have two people becoming one when all the cards
are on the table, when a woman is no longer hiding her
character from her man or a man from his woman. You
will never get a true marriage until a man knows all that
is in his woman, for good or evil. And the same with the
woman in regard to the man. Until all that is contemptible
in your man is seen not with blind eyes but with open
eyes, you are not going to gain access to the thrill and the
beauty of a fulfilled relationship.

Now the types of character armour adopted by a couple
to avoid ultimate confrontation in marriage are many:
these will be discussed later. What I want to show now is
how it can happen that people come to marriage with
various fixations or hang-ups in their characters and how
the marriage relationship can in fact help people to grow

out of these in much the same way as a psycho-analyst would help them. The danger in writing like this is that half my readers could attack their wives or husbands and say: 'I told you so. . . . You've been waiting for this, and now you've got it!' Thus I may be putting ammunition in the hands of some who have been just waiting round for the opportunity. But we must remember that most marriages will have the problems I talk about to a greater or lesser extent and the only way out of these is honesty and talking to one another. And if my book makes people talk to one another I will be happy.

Now what are some of these distortions of character which may exist in people when they come to marriage, and how do they arise? The first thing to remember is that they arise from the exaggeration of certain traits in people, traits which every normal person has, and this exaggeration very often is the result of some 'hitch' in the person's upbringing, some suppression or distortion caused by rigid or authoritarian or selfish parents.

Take the case of two types of behaviour which appear at certain stages in all young children—exhibitionism and peeping. The exhibition instinct appears when the child becomes first aware of itself, because a child only gradually gets to know itself and realise that it is different and separate from its surroundings. And this is an amazing realisation for the child; it's really no wonder he wants to exhibit this discovery to the people around him. His behaviour at this stage is saying in effect something like: 'Here I am; aren't I amazing, marvellous. You didn't realise what an extraordinary fellow you had here, did you?' And, of course, the child displays all of himself, a circumstance which causes all sorts of discomfiture if he belongs to one of those middle-class, hypocritical families who are shocked by anything so natural and innocent. Because it is natural, innocent, and very important for the development of the child's idea of himself. If a child is prevented from going through this phase in a normal manner, it seems reasonable to expect such suppression to affect his future behaviour. For example, take the case of a woman who, when she was small, was never allowed to express herself in any sort of display which is so important to young children. A man who marries such a woman may find that her need to show off affects everything she does. Her dress bill is exorbitant; she will always want to move house to a 'better' district. A man married to such a woman is chasing a 'will o' the wisp' because she is driven by an impulse which she herself doesn't understand. Sometimes it takes a gross form of dressing in the most atrocious clothes or talking loudly so as to attract everyone's attention. A man who was excessively exhibitionist might, for example, bankrupt himself acquiring stocks which he couldn't afford. I knew one such who in the end, when the crash came, couldn't face it; he committed suicide.

Behind all this distortion is the simple human urge to be sure of oneself by getting a little recognition from others. The exhibitionist instinct is the very thing that spurs on actors, artists, and such people to behave creatively. So you see, it is a very important aspect of every human being. But if it is blocked up right from the start by stuffy parents, it can become distorted and exaggerated later on. The little child when he displays himself is looking for assessment from others to help him know himself. If he doesn't get his feedback he may become permanently anxious about his own identity.

Another tendency in young children which must be understood is the 'peeping' instinct, which in the adult is the real basis of all types of research activities. You can imagine the effect on a child if his parents refuse to allow him to explore. The trouble is that quite often his exploration gets to the point where the little 'secrets' of the parents are threatened. For example, what does one do to a child who is found peeping in the keyhole when Mammy is taking a bath? The problem is to teach the child to be selective in his 'peeping' rather than suppress it altogether. If peeping or exploration is punished, all sorts of learning in the future may become a furtive and guilt-ridden experience. And yet this 'exploratory' tendency is the source of all mental growth.

Everyone nowadays knows about the 'aggressive' instinct in man, a part of the self-preservation instinct. But if this instinct becomes swollen and selfish, it can lead to the need to eradicate everything outside of the self. Thus a wife will tolerate her husband to the extent that he adapts himself to her and her ways. A husband, on the other hand, wants an adaptation from her to his ways and can only stand her if she makes such an adaptation. This comes from an exaggeration of the self-preservation instinct and can lead to continual aggression against the other party, making married life an unending misery.

These are only a few of the many types of distortions of character which can occur. Behind them all though is basically the same mechanism, some area of the personality which became either suppressed or exaggerated by an unfavourable childhood environment. But the real problem in this is the many guises adopted by individuals to cover up such a deficiency—what kind of character armour is used to hide the real source of the trouble. This is what makes it difficult for some married couples to understand the real cause of their conflicts. A person who has been mentally hurt in his childhood in some of these ways is like a knight in armour in his own beleagured castle, surrounded by the moat of his own defences and very difficult to get at. For example, analysts have found that when a person has the sort of unresolved conflicts within himself that we have been talking about, he creates spurious behaviour patterns to cover them up. Every one of us suppresses some things about ourselves that we might be ashamed of; the growling primitive is always there within us. In the marriage relationship everything comes out, but the analysts have found that what comes out may not give much indication of the real conflicts within. Just like the medieval knights clothed themselves in armour, people who have repressed things often develop traits which are completely opposite to the things they have repressed. For example, a person with strong hate impulses might become a pacifist and join pacifist societies and go out and give talks on pacifism and really believe he was a man of peace. Or a person who wished to display and show himself off would become completely humble

and shy in front of everybody so that you really would
think that that was his real self. This sort of substitution makes it more difficult to understand such people.
Also, a person who has got such a false armour-plated
ego has the tendency not to be mobile of spirit and not to
be delicately aware of changes in other people. He is
stilted and narrow and limited, and his life is often an
impoverished life. He does not really feel or know or
have the movements that belong to the really vital person
and, therefore, he suffers enormously. You will meet some
of these people in churches, religious people, very rigid,
very static, very determined to keep the Ten Command-
ments, very careful to do all the things that are right, to
pay their bills correctly, to be not like other men are. But
their rigidity is the give-away even if their particular
avocation is not. And because of this sort of substitution,
when confrontation occurs in marriage the things said
may give no indication whatever of the real problem. I
want to outline now how psychoanalysis goes about getting at the real cause of such conflicts and I will finish by
showing that the very same thing can be achieved in the
home by the marriage partners themselves, if they are
prepared to make the effort.

All the truly fine analysts in Europe or America have
expressed in similar words the idea that the one essential in an analyst is love; without love you cannot heal.
You can't heal just because you do the studies. You can't
heal because you learn the theory or even the practice.
Unless you can convey a real sense of concern to a disturbed person, he will not risk digging into his unconscious
for he will have a dread that you will shatter him. So the
analyst must proceed with care and patience. An analyst
who hurries with his job may please the finances of his
patient but he will not achieve any permanent curative
influence on the personality. For example, Freud would
never take a person in training as an analyst just because
he was clever or because he was a doctor. As a matter of
fact, he thought that training as a doctor often made you
shut your eyes to the psychological or spiritual side of personality. He claimed that people who were going to anal-

yse should first of all be analysed themselves, so that they knew how it felt; second, they should be broad-minded and tolerant people; and third, they should be cultured people in the sense that they could take in the whole ambit of humanity, that they understand in some measure the human race and the purposes that lie at the heart of humanity. The central factor in the analyst's healing is love. By love I mean the spiritual capacity to give another person utter freedom to say whatever they feel like saying without condemnation. Given this capacity and the required insight, the analyst can allow the patient to act out the problems or conflicts which are causing his anguish.

The analyst is like a person sitting in a theatre watching a drama, but he must maintain a detached and clearly intellectual mind. It is not easy; it requires all the forces of a creative personality to do it; it requires great patience and understanding; it requires graciousness and simplicity of heart so that he forgets about himself and becomes absorbed in the patient's problems. When he does this, he can endure any eruptions that occur. In this way, the patient learns that he can say anything without fear of reprisal, that he can let all his pent-up emotions flow out without fear. The analyst pays attention patiently in the manner in which the patient's parents failed to do long ago.

Now I find that in most cases the course of analysis follows a certain pattern. At first, things are friendly and indeed female patients may even fall in love with you for a while. This is the positive phase. Because you listen so patiently, you are an angel out of heaven sent; there is no one so kind as you, no one so understanding, no one so competent to understand the sensitivities of a man or a woman. Things go very smoothly; you seem to be splendidly successful as an analyst. But when that atmosphere develops, you may be quite sure that not very far behind there is a tiger in the aeroplane. You may be flying along splendidly, when suddenly there is a heavy paw on your shoulder and you come face to face with wild eyes and growling teeth; the negative phase has commenced. Now the thing to remember about this negative phase is that it is full of hope. When it occurs the cure has started. This phase is the renaissance, the awakening of memories super-charged with emotion that belong to the buried past. But the point is that the person is not aware that they are acting out their unconscious feelings in this way. They may seize on something trivial in the therapeutic situation and have a huge quarrel about it. But all the time the emotion displayed has nothing to do with you; it is the release of emotions that have been suppressed in the past. One of the illustrations I often give of this phase is that of the story of an underground river which was discovered some years ago in Derbyshire. In order to find where it went, people stained the waters red and watched all the local rivers to see which one became red. Something similar happens in the negative phase of analysis. An immense river of emotion belonging to a prior situation is transferred to the person of the analyst. This makes it difficult for ladies to be analysts because the abuse of the analyst during this phase can be quite vicious. For example, a lady analyst has had it said to her: 'You know, you really have very ugly teeth; God knows why you don't go and get them fixed! And as for your shoes, yuk! I'd hate to see the feet which come out of those shoes with their corns and knubbly toes! No wonder you're not married; God, no wonder!' . . . and so on. A number of ladies who started out quite well as analysts had to give up because this negative phase became too difficult, too disturbing. They started to hit back. And this is the temptation facing every analyst, to react in a similarly emotional and vicious way to the patient. So you have got to learn that serene and quiet detachment which allows you a tender and intellectual understanding of the situation. The analyst has got to be such a person that the patient feels increasingly that he can give up conscious attempts to control himself and then finds to his own amazing relief that he can unconsciously go loose. He can unconsciously transfer his feeling, and the analyst becomes the recipient of both intensely hostile and critical judgments and also affectionate and warm judgments. The analyst's job is to receive both of these, not in a spirit of carelessness or aloofness, but in a spirit of human understanding so that the child in the person can reawaken, so that the person can abandon his grown-up-ness for a half hour with the analyst, learn more and more to receive his own childhood into himself and be a naughty or good little child just as he likes in relation to the analyst. For instance, if a patient hits me in the chest (which they've done), or smacks my face (which they've done), or tries to choke me (which they've done), they can't any more say this action hasn't taken place. Because I say to them, here, now is a proof of what you're talking about. You are now acting in this way. I never harmed you, I never did this to you: you are doing it. And it is my pleasant or unpleasant duty to call attention to the fact that this educated gentleman or lady is capable of punching me, or smacking my face, or pulling tongues at me, or swearing at me, or stamping her feet at me, or flinging cushions at me, or behaving in other ways that very gentle ladies can under certain circumstances. The analyst who is the recipient of these things then discovers humanity as humanity is. But it doesn't end there, for the job of the analyst is to point out the reality of the situation. And if the analyst keeps his balance in the job, sooner or later he strikes the infantile memories, and the woman or man can suddenly remember the experiences of shame, the experiences of pain, the experiences of jealousy, of envy, of malice, which belong to their early days. And they discover an extraordinary opening of their mind, and how profound and intense womanhood is and manhood is; how rooted we all are in fundamental, primal feeling: how everyone of us is related to the ape, as we are to the angels. Evolutionally we contain everything, the high and the low. And the wonderful thing is that if the patient has the courage to face his own childhood in this way, he will go through a process of growing up. For that's the analyst's job. To see that the patient gradually grows up from the age of three or four to the age of five or six, seven or eight, nine or ten, until a healthy person can be restored to the fullness of her femininity, or the fullness of his masculinity, as the case may be.

Now the interesting thing is that these same processes can and do occur in many marriages; the partners can and should act the role of analyst for each other. Even the phases of a typical course of analysis occur in the marriage relationship. When you first get married, the same positive phase occurs. Your wife is an angel; she is never angry and does all the right things. Your husband is so understanding; when you get a bit ratty, he's so calm and helpful, so capable—when the lock wanted a bit of mending the other day he straightaway went and mended it (I have seen other men wait for months). So in the early days of a marriage everything goes swimmingly; but this positive phase is nourishing your souls with an elusive treachery. For after a while, some tiny unimportant event suddenly reveals the tigress in your damsel. Some simple occurrence reveals the pig-like qualities of your prince and you find yourself looking for trotters down where his shoes are. And this gradually mounts up so that you go through several weeks of unbelievable shattering. You go around with baggy eyes and wander from flat to shop in total misery, dragging a bag, and your husband begins to talk to his pals about how hard life is and so on. What is happening of course is that the negative phase is emerging. And just as in analysis, this is a real cause for hope, because it is a sign that you are treating the marriage as a depth situation in which you are beginning to display your real personalities to one another. Although the first phase is replete with delights and comforts, the real ability to build a marriage shows when the negative phase arrives and the raw and not very well smoothed out aspects of the personalities come out into the open. The reason that marriages fail at this point is that the partners fail to adopt the passive attitude which the analyst attempts to maintain. Instead they hit back at something which really wasn't aimed at them in the first place. If each of them in their turn could preserve that tender gentle receptivity that comes on the one hand from some insight into the whole business and on the other from a love that is prepared to make the effort, this is the real way to produce a truly Christian marriage, but I have not met any priests or clergymen who approached it in this manner.

And just as with the analyst, the essential element at this stage is that of love. When a man finds himself married to a woman who is upset or a wife finds herself attached to a man who is disturbed, if you have any sense of religion, any real love-foundation, you wait prayerfully and without recriminations. Just as you would go into a quiet forest to find the city's noise fading, you put a silent distance between yourself and your beloved which, no matter what they say or do, prevents you from the danger of recrimination.

And you learn that whatever your beloved may do, whatever she may say, whatever she may scornfully fling at you, you will remain in the quietness of your heart attached to her without any withdrawal, but at the same time detached from the brutality of an emotional reaction. You will not withdraw from her in a self-righteous defence, and you will not abandon her. In the quiet recess of your own heart you will gather the strength that is not your strength but is the strength of God. And viewed from that inner level of high beauty and holiness, you will not be talking at her. In fact you might not say much, but you will be talking to her and not at her. And you will find yourself filled with understanding and pity, and see that you are beholding a girl growing. In the same way, when a woman is prepared to stand by and allow her husband to grow and not trip him up at every step with recrimination, she is guaranteeing not only his growth, but their mutual growth and the growth of their marriage.

Ultimately this is achieved by the fires of love. Love is not an emotion, a goo-goo feeling; it is a sincere and fearless intellectual look at the woman of your life or the man of your life. It is only when you have seen it with the clear intellectual light of creative love, it is only then that you are moved to concern.

This is the atmosphere that creates holy marriage, holy marriage as opposed to marriage. Holy marriage is marriage in which the woman is wild as ever she has been, but nonetheless can feel secure. She can bring to you all her wildness unafraid, for your strength is not going to be a fist to smash her face or a sneer to break her heart. Your strength is the overwhelming tenderness that means constancy to her. She can be undefended before you, for you are worthy of that non-defence. And when your woman can come to you undefended, holding nothing back, hiding nothing, showing everything that she is capable of in bitchiness and everything else, it is only then that you catch the vision of her transcendent beauty. It is only then that you hold up to her the image of what she truly is and in your love words create the image that she knows she is, and she becomes what you dream of her—for your dream is the truth.

Then you have the glorious experience of telepathic love, the love where your whole being flows telepathically into the utmost depth of the other, and the utmost depth of the other flows back into you, and you commingle in transcendent rapture. You are both ennobled and exalted, you are both transfigured and lifted up, you both see in each other the splendour of the gods and the glory of the morning. You see in each other that profound strength that can nurse all the sorrows of creation to the achievement of the victory of evolution and the victory of life. For marriage offers the jungle to live in to find splendour of the Kingdom of Heaven. And it is out of the rapture of that splendour that babies are truly conceived and born, not out of the sensuality of the moment. In this way, your mating becomes truly a sacrament.

Marriage offers this tremendous opportunity, this tremendous joy, this tremendous fulfilment. There is no ambition of pride, there is no ambition of intellect, there is no ambition of science or of philosophy or of poetry equal to this. A man loses himself in his woman, loses all his egotism, loses all his narcissism, and she loses hers in him, and they intertwine and they interblend and the music of the spheres sings through their rapture. Marriage is not one of life's necessary compromises; it is the most sublime occasion for personal growth that man or woman can encounter. And this is our inheritance, this is our

gift. This is what we may be if we will dare—married.
This is a thing which makes you reach old age without
fear, reach old age with joy in your heart, without any
terror of death. You are carrying on that which transcends your own life, for you reach into the ages to come.

JEKYLL
AND
HYDE

CHAPTER THREE

When people first fall in love, they are attracted in very mysterious ways. And although people think of Freud as a hardheaded man of science, he had in fact the very beautiful conception of love as a man and a woman forming one cell of life. Each man or woman is a separate half and sometimes one of the halves may be at the other end of the world. But, by some mysterious force, they gravitate towards one another until they meet. When they look back on it later and trace how they met and by what apparent accidents they met, they find it very mysterious; thus the most fundamental bonds of life are formed apparently by accident. Emerson would not agree with this doctrine of accidents; he maintained that God worked through accidents and that great men always trust themselves childlike to the genius of their age, to the connection of persons, to the connection of events, believing that divine providence works thereby. So, although marriages where people gravitated towards one another in some mysterious way seem to be accidental occurrences, Freud saw them as rooted in something very profound. However the process of being married does not always run too smoothly. What happens? Well, let's take a look at how the story goes!

When young lovers first meet each other, they are attracted by the beauty, or the virility, or the strength, or the imagination or the audacity of the other, or indeed any of the qualitiies that draw men and women together. And I think it is true to say, that from that time on, the girl does her best to dress as nicely as she can; she may develop a new interest in jewellery; she never worried too much before about makeup, but now she considers her appearance not quite consistent with her new personality, so she becomes more particular about how she looks. The boy also develops a concern for his appearance, to the amazement of his parents. And his pals are amazed to see him walking around, holding hands with his girl who flings her locks back and parades with a seraphic audacity. Before going out to meet him, the girl wonders whether she should wear a mini or not; she's not quite sure: 'Will he think I'm forward? No, I don't think so! Anyway I've got very nice legs and why shouldn't I show them.' So she hands out half a week's wages for a new mini and presents herself full of delight and hope to her fellow. About this time too, his parents begin to notice and to wonder who she is and who are her people? And her parents also begin investigations and maybe conflict develops, and the beautiful girl, whom the boy only sees as the essence of gentleness, becomes quite bitchy with her mother. But they surmount these difficulties and things progress.

Then one night he is fifteen minutes late for a date. When he arrives her little lips are not smiling; they are tightly drawn and pale. 'I'm sorry, I missed the bus.' 'Did you?' she replies, and a cold shiver runs up and down his spine. This is a new development, an aspect of his girl which he hadn't seen before. And as well as that, he has another problem; he's only got a few bob to spare to buy a bite after the show. So he has nothing himself and becomes a Gandhi so she can have something. But he's not quite satisfied with the situation. So gradually the two lovers start seeing things in each other which they hadn't seen before. But they do their best to shut their eyes to each other's delinquencies and see only each other's good points, right through to the usual respectable marriage, where all the telegrams are read and the toasts are drunk. And off they go to the honeymoon.

Well, the moon of honey, the moon of phantasm and joy, the thrill of entering at last into the ineffable secret is delicious—at first. But within a couple of days....

'Don't speak to me...'

Well! His wife's bosom was very beautiful but her back is not quite so nice, especially if it is deliberately presented! And so the little episodes occur and before long your man is saying to himself, 'God I wish this was over and I could get back to work!' And milady, pondering on the situation at night, says to herself, 'He's not as nice as I thought he was...a bit sour!' So, the real unveiling is starting to take place. They face each other with increasing irritability, an increasing sense of failure. As he sits across the breakfast table from her, he says to himself, 'Have I got to sit opposite this for fifty years?' And when she asks him what he was thinking of he says, 'Oh, I was just thinking how wonderful your hair is, darling!' And so the little hypocrisies creep in to maintain the fiction of a perfect marriage. And if he only knew she was just thinking to herself, 'Flat face, that's what you are! Flat face.' But she doesn't say that! She says, very nicely, 'I was thinking, dear, of your father.' And things sometimes get so bad that eventually, if the pretence is kept up, they end up going to marriage counsellors. And I'm afraid a lot of marriage counsels are staffed by old duffers with little wisdom and less sexual vitality, who offer little more than clichés appropriate to each case. 'All you've got to remember, dear, when you marry a man, is to put up with him; you've got to put up with him.' And the girl who dreamt of having a husband who would take her arm in trouble and say, 'Darling, lean on me,' finds that now she has someone she just must 'put up with'! And the man for his part, can't understand how the little cat who is acting up like this was once a sweet girl with beautiful hair falling over her shoulders, who used to say, 'Yes, Percy dear.'

Now what's behind this drastic deterioration in the relationship?

Everyone deep down has a basic selfishness, which changes as we mature, that is, if we mature. It doesn't matter how beautiful you've grown; it doesn't matter how much philosophy you've read; it doesn't matter how many poems you can quote by heart or whether you can read the Bible backwards. It makes no difference. In other words, every little girl and boy down in the roots of their being is in love with one person only—themselves. And how that self grows depends enormously on the parental influence. If the parents are kind and cultured and loving and friendly, this selfishness will grow into a very healthy and natural condition of self-love which then overflows from the self out to others. But the home may be a place where the child's liberties are constantly assailed, where the child's temper is not allowed any expression, because the goody-goody parents want sweet, innocent, wee children. And of course there is no such a thing. In such homes where parents do not allow their children to express themselves, the love of the child turns back on itself. And we must remember that children naturally have an immense love for their parents. And they must express this; in fact, they must be allowed to express all their feelings honestly. For example, one child can be quite jealous when another is born.

I want you to understand what a hard thing it is for a little child of two or three to have a little baby come into the house and claim all the attention—to understand the agony of that child, all the jealousy, envy, that is in that child. But often the child is not allowed to express his feelings. 'Be quiet! You mustn't be angry! God doesn't want you to be angry.' So the child is quiet because children are afraid when grownups are angry with them. So the child hides its feelings and presents a false front to those around it.

Now, many parents are hypocrites, demanding standards of life from children which they can't live up to. And because they do this, many people grow up suffering from an ingrown love. And just like the tide of the sea can draw back into itself, leaving all the sands desolate and without water, so the personality can leave the exterior world and focus within itself hatreds and malices. But it does it so cleverly that one would not suspect it.

Now a person in this condition is utterly selfish. He basically loves no one but himself. But in the intimacy of the marriage relationship, this selfishness is unearthed. And when it is, people can become like animals, literally like wild beasts, with the most unbelievable, torrential powers. It was bad enough when they were young to be packed with unexpressed hate; but to be packed with unexpressed hate when you've got a fully developed muscularity, when you've got a fully developed mind, a fully developed will and emotion, means that you've got the wildest, most wordless, most angry, most foul things fighting in your heart. And you've got to pretend that you haven't because society does not allow sincerity, society does not allow honesty. But the result is that when such people are forced to live together, they really bang against each other.

This brings us to the pith of the marriage: marriage isn't worth one penny, until one or the other partner has the courage to strike into the fundamental selfishness of the other and lay it bare, and fight the fight that is necessary to bring one's mate to reality with themselves, to cleave all this pretence, this shadowy show, and let the hate and the anger expose itself. And if the man, for example, has any insight into the situation, he will know that although his wife hurls all sorts of abuse at him, that this is her salvation. He is seeing the things that wounded her most, and she is finding release by flinging them at him. And this is the cross of a Christian marriage, to accept her and not to abandon her. And so the true man and the true woman burn into each other.

Instead of making a path to each other in this way, sometimes the woman goes out and tells her friends over a cup of tea or he tells the lads over a pint. Support parties for the two sides are formed and the whole of their private life is thrown open to the public. But a brave man or a brave woman goes to nobody but to the woman who has disturbed them or the man who has disturbed them. They are determined to split the very atom of life in order

to get at the subatomic energy that lies within the heart
of the people who are bound to them. But such bravery
must be rooted in love. If it is not rooted in love and you
dare to disturb the growling beast, you will be destroyed
by it.

This brave acceptance of the danger of marriage is the
reality of love. If you face it, then your wife or your husband lays bare everything that is in him. And this calls
forth from you the basic things in you and you are naked
opposite each other, two wild things of the primeval forest, with all the palaeolithic and neolithic elements that
belonged to primitive man outpouring in this home of
yours.

There is a grief in the human heart, there is something
that comes into a man when he sees his woman thus exposed, there is an infinite pity that comes over his soul,
for he sees that this woman of his is not so much rebelling against him, and rebelling against life, as she is revealing the unfulfilled yearnings of her childhood. She is
lost, in need of care and guidance. She needs a man whose
profound, gentle love faces her ruthlessness, who takes
her contempt without being contemptuous, her hate without hating, her wildness without going wild himself. In
this way he will enfold his woman, so that she can genuinely break down and weep. And instead of the punishment which she had learned to expect, she meets the concern which is in every man if you look for it, in the centre
of his being. And she meets not man the brute, but the
grown-up, authentic, adult man who allows her to display
her dread and her fear and her frightful loneliness. But
he won't do it with many words, not even with poetic
words of love: he'll do it with the gentle touch on the
cheek or a gentle touch on the hand or a slight pat on the
head, while his voice conveys his profound concern for
his mate, an utter ache to feel her, and to lift her out of
her self-possession. And it's the same with a woman. For
when she is faced with the brutality and ruthlessness of
an egoistic man, she is faced with one of the most hellish
things anyone can face on earth. But if she maintains
her femininity, she will find her man. If she lets him feel

the truth, that part of him is only a child who long ago
was terribly wounded, she will keep him.

The true marriage is the marriage that transcends this
struggle. And in our church, the Anglican church, we put
it in these words: that 'I take thee to be my lawful wed-
ded wife, to have and to hold, from this day forward, for
better for worse, for richer for poorer, in sickness and in
health, to love and to cherish till death us do part.' (*Book
of Common Prayer*). But any man who has ever loved a
woman knows quite well death doesn't part. You can
look into the eyes of your woman, and as you grow older
and death gets nearer to you, you are not frightened by
death, you are not overwhelmed by it, and you are not
made sorrowful and depressed, for you see death as the
door to eternal life. Just like the chick comes out of the
shell: when it first is in the shell you could not understand its shape or its form, but when the shell breaks and
the little chick is released, then you understand the use of
its legs, of its beak, of its wings, all the things that made
no sense before. And we are like the chick inside the shell.
But there comes a period when we break the shell; the
shell is shattered, somehow or other, and those of us who
have tied ourselves to our woman discover that although
the body and the sex of the body tie us to our woman, the
divine sex of the spirit is a million times more profound.
The spiritual, mystical, sexual love of man for woman, and
woman for man, in its ineffable beauty and excellence,
ties us tighter than life itself until, although the physical
is so majestic and so lovely, it is as naught beside this
rapturous, utterly safe bond that you feel binds you to
your mate. Through every vicissitude of life, he or she
will stand with you, and hold to you, and hold your hand
at the moment of death, if they are there. And this is the
victory of marriage, and this is the only foundation of human society. But it is from those fundamentally founded
marriages that children are born in beauty, and reared
in goodness and kindness and gentleness. From such marriages a new age is born, new children with the new vision, with a new freedom, with a new light, who in turn
have their children, and their freedom, and so on, for a

thousand generations. It is in our power, by our courage, by our determination, to found our marriage in eternity and transform history by the way we transform the lives of little children who come under our care, if God gives us little children.

The only thing that I know which matters in life is love. Jesus, when he was asked about adultery, didn't say that adultery was people living together who weren't married. He said, 'He that lusteth after a woman in his spirit has already committed adultery.' Therefore if a man lusts after his wife, he commits adultery every time he makes love to her. If he makes love to his wife physically for any other reason except out of a spiritual and loving attraction to her at that moment, it is adultery. Jesus set very high standards for marriage indeed!

CRESCENDO

CHAPTER FOUR

Music began with melody, a simple, single tune. Probably the first musical instruments were the reed instruments. Man, having a plaintive or tender message to declare, found in the human voice and in the reed instrument an expression of his inner spiritual life. So right from the beginning we find that music is tied intimately to the spirit of man, to his very essence.

The interesting thing is that as man set out to express himself in music, like a traveller along a main country road, more and more he had a tendency to turn off the main road and explore the surrounding countryside. As a result, he developed not only melody but the harmonies and discords of music.

But music is not free. It is limited to the few octaves which the human ear can hear. Within these octaves man explores the depth of the human spirit, the resonances of his nature. For example, he finds that different types of instruments seem to express different aspects of his being. Brasses, reeds, and percussion all affect him in different ways. And the musical conductor is like a man who advances his army along a main road but also deploys various sections of his orchestra into the surrounding countryside.

Sir Thomas Beecham once said that it doesn't matter how fantastic, complicated, or intellectual music may be, that ultimately it is rooted in the melody. And if you do not keep to the melody and confine all your marvellous instruments of expression to a deeper reading of the melody, you are becoming a mathematician and not a musician. Some modern musicians are just that. They've learned how to construct chords and discords, assonances, consonances, and so on, in a brilliant, intellectual way, and they fling them in every direction; but there is no fundamental movement, no fundamental drive, and no fundamental life-meaning in it. Sibelius, Beethoven, and Wagner with their musical storms were well aware that their adventures into overtone, counterpoint, harmony, and discord must always be an expression in sound of the human spirit. So music above all else is a form of communication, a very deep and intimate form. And the most fundamental aspect of this communication is the melody.

Now before I go on to discuss the relevance of all this to marriage, I want to make a point. It is important to remember that many of the deepest and most profound matings of men and women in this world have not been consummated in marriage; indeed some of them have had to fight alongside tragedies of marriage. I would not hurt or insult a mighty thing like human mating by limiting it to those fortunate few people who have been able to bring their mating to a successful and holy marriage which is, of course, the ideal thing.

But now back to music. The simplest form of harmony is the unison, that is, when you play two notes, one an octave above the other, and your ear tells you they fit very well together. Now that is how nearly all marriages and matings begin. We begin by being attracted to someone who is like ourselves with whom we have an affinity. In some mysterious way, this person affects us profoundly and we affect them. And some of the sweetest and most melodious love relations are based on that simple kind of unison, which is very like the shepherd's song in primitive pastoral poetry. The atmosphere is peaceful; there's no struggle, no quarrel because the partners are so like

each other they are harmonised or unified. And this is
the sort of thing we all seek, whether we know it or not,
when we fall in love or marry. We look for the one who
we feel is our other self.

After the octaves in music, the next basic harmonies
are combinations of C and G, and G and D, and E and
B, and so on. There is a sense of comfort in these combinations especially if you prolong them on a violin or an
organ, so that you experience all the overtones or harmonies. Many simple hymns use these harmonies. There
is no conflict at all; everything is cherubic and happy.
And when we sing them we feel as if we are almost already in that lovely melodious heaven that we sing about.
And the relationship of some couples is like that all their
lives. They first join together in unison and remain no
further apart for the rest of their lives than these harmonies, never searching out the depths of each other.

Browning the poet once said, 'Why rush the discords in
but that harmony may be prized?' But I think there is
more to adventures in music than just that. The great
composers create discords because they sense the spiritual
strife of man. In flinging discords in gigantic form into
his music, a man like Sibelius is not doing it solely that
harmony should be prized. He is searching out the potential of sound; he is refusing to accept the convention
that you've got to be harmonic in order to be musical. On
the other hand, if there is no resolution in the music (and
in some modern music there is no resolution), the human
spirit feels defeated. There is a feeling that the impulse
has gone beyond the intelligence; that some immense order of emotion has been awakened which leaves the heart
restless. The great masters take us into these depths and
search out the terrors and majesties and madnesses of the
human soul. They wake us out of the lethargy of the
commonplace in which we do little more than proceed
endlessly in a straight line. They make us aware of forces
within ourselves so that we feel if we could only understand them, if we could only embrace these discords, we
would be possessed of immense power.

When men and women first encounter each other, they

follow the conventional muse of love, octaval unions which
then blend into hymn-sweet harmonies. But you can be
sure of one thing—that however beautiful a woman is,
she is a bitch, and if you have never found that out, you
have never found a woman. The average man is afraid
of meeting the bitch and makes all kinds of evasive melodious manoeuvres to avoid a marrowbone confrontation.
In the same way, a man looks nice and strong and hand-
some until the brute in him is laid bare. Most relationships start out in unison and then go on to the simple
harmonies. But if they're worth anything at all, they
then plunge into the excitement and dangers and pain of
the discords, the unmasking of the brute and the bitch
that are in every man and woman.

Of course if we're women, we don't see it this way. We
believe ourselves to be innocent, beautiful little things
who, though misunderstood, are prepared to bear this
lonely cross for the rest of our days. On the other hand,
if we are men, having read poetry and imbued ourselves
with delicate feminine music, we are appalled to find a
vicious little tigress under our roof. We retreat and brood
over it and feel awfully hurt. How can she lie there like
that all night and not put her arms around us? And so
it goes on like that for two, maybe three, nights and nothing doing! The crucifying one and the crucified lie together with miles of silence between them. And all the
while, the immense forces that created that silence can
be harnessed and the discords can be resolved into the most
ravishing music, if the couple only knew. And just as
the great composers long ago left behind the idea of a
quick and easy resolution in music, so a married couple
must learn that discords are the prelude to the most delicious harmonies. When you arrive home, how happy
you are depends on where you've been. Unless you discover these discords and surmount them, your marriage
won't grow. Because in the absence of the truth, a lady
likes to think that she is sweet, gentle, patient, and long-
suffering. And her husband likes to think that it's almost
like a Christian mission that he has got to keep going;
and in the meantime, he casts his eye over all the other

beautiful women passing to and fro, all more sweet and all more beautiful than the one he's stuck with.

One of the most fundamental things that must happen in any marriage is that the couple must have the courage to face the ultimate depths of each other. Few of us come to marriage with a well-balanced personality. And we must have the honesty and sincerity to realise this. And often enough when a woman acts up, what she wants is not consolation, she doesn't want to be told she's pretty; she wants to be told what a man will tell her whether it's strong or piteous or angry or tender. She wants the feeling that it is a man talking to her, not a damned coward who recoils at the sight of her fangs. Even when a woman is fighting you like hell, she wants to know that at the right moment at the crisis you are not going to sell the pass or give way. She must feel that you will stand up for what you believe is true or just, even though she may never let you know this and may not even know it herself.

In the same way, when a man comes to a woman with a tender masculine feeling, he doesn't want to be faced with an amazon! The trouble is that in our sophisticated civilisation, the only time men and women speak honestly to one another is when brothers and sisters are scratching each other's eyes and pulling each other's hair. Apart from that, there seems to be some sort of conspiracy not to declare one's real emotion.

Now this honesty business isn't as easy as it might seem at first. You tell her the truth and there's no apparent reaction. So you keep going. Lips tighten a bit, she looks out the window and says, 'Go on!' Now when a woman says, 'Go on!' she means 'Shut up!' But this is the point at which a man must keep going, right on to the explosion. And God help the man who was under the impression that women are the weaker sex. No man who has ever slept with a woman or fought with her ever believed such nonsense. But if you have the courage to flame your differences, to explore the discords, you will discover the mystery of sex. And just as the great musicians would never have written such wonderful music if they had not struggled through oceans and continents of discords, so we must struggle to find truth and light in our relationships as man and woman. A man and woman know so little about each other even after they have slept with each other for years. Because I think that the end of it all is mystery. Instead of arriving at knowledge as you thought and as sex books will tell you, you discover the whole thing is a mystery. All my life I have studied it and I am now seventy-two but I have more sense of the mystery of life than I had when I was twenty. As my experience grew my knowledge seemed to disappear. When a man and a woman get really close to one another, there is nothing to say, nothing to explain.

In all this, however, I think it is bad for a man to dominate a woman but it is even worse if he lets her dominate him. He must have the courage to discover her, to lead her, to find out what makes her tick. For example, I have always said that spring and autumn are the time to give your wife a prescription in the form of clothes, not in terms of medication. She won't thank you for the medication, but she will have far fewer headaches if she gets some extra clothes. Not many men understand how important a part of woman's being is display. And this is not a question of simply putting on different dresses. It is a question of speech. A woman talks to men this way, in endless variety if she gets the chance. A woman declares herself far more in her dress than in her undress. And you can't understand the mystery of the undress until you know the mystery of the dress. A woman does not dress herself idly. When she does so, she has a very clear eye on the person she loves. She has a very clear spiritual understanding of the persons who concern her. All ladies would like to have a bigger wardrobe than they have got. It is not a matter of spending, either; it is a question of initiating her personality, of declaring herself. But men don't understand this. And they hate paying out money for clothes, although they don't mind spending it on tobacco or beer or a sweep ticket. But suggest spending six guineas on a new dress and they go through the roof! Just watch a lady doing herself up. Her dressing-table is her altar and the whole process is like a religious

ritual: she surrounds herself with this and that before
she begins, arranging everything in proper order; a whole
procedure has to be gone through. And if you understand
her, you won't interrupt the procedure but you'll sit back
and enjoy it, because it's all part of the spiritual process
of being a woman.

On the other hand, what about men? Shakespeare once
said: 'Men were deceivers ever, one foot in sea and one
on shore, To one thing constant never. Then sigh not so,
But let them go, And be you blithe and bonny...' Supposing a pretty girl crosses the road with fifty married
men and fifty single men looking on! How many pairs
of eyes do you think follow the lady? Men have roving
eyes and if a woman doesn't know that she will never contain her man. Men with their imagination are very easily
attracted by beauty; they are easily attracted by the
form of beauty, easily allured. But I assure you that is
on the surface only. Men are not fools; when trouble
comes, when things go wrong, they come every time to
the fundamental woman. And there is always a fundamental woman. This is why it is foolish to worry when
their eyes wander, when they praise another woman.
You shouldn't spend jealous days moping or troubling
yourself. Because a wandering eye is part of man's nature and it is the same wandering eye which will rest on
you so lovingly when you dress for him. And this is the
real problem between men and women. These differences,
problems, discords must be admitted and encountered
squarely, because it is out of the discords that the ultimate concords, the ultimate harmonies of life are made.

I can't imagine anyone more different from myself than
my wife; I can't see any likeness between us. So you
would be quite mistaken if you thought that we have
achieved the love that we have by simple unison or even
more complicated harmonies. I have fought my woman
with whatever sincerity is in me and I have encouraged
her to fight me, because only through such searchings,
through such discords do you come across the hidden
splendours that lie in each other. This may not be possible
for people who think marriage consists of being sweet

and good and never quarrelling. But if a man is a man, it is wrong for him to be bound by convention or dominated by his woman. It is cowardly and wrong for a man to let a woman trespass on his being to the point that he daren't declare what he thinks and feels and knows. And if this means you run the risk of losing your mate then sometimes this card must be thrown down in the life-struggle. Even if you risk losing the person you love most on earth you must take that ultimate risk! And my experience is that when you take that ultimate risk it is not in vain. Instead, the relationship grows in delight and power and affection and delicacy as the days go by. For example, I think the menopause in both men and women occurs far too early and is much more significant than it should be. And the reason is that so many people fail to achieve this harmony to face and surmount the challenge of discord in the marriage relationship. And menopause becomes an excuse for the dying emotional fires which have not been allowed to blaze up and fuse the partners together in the white heat of ultimate confrontation. All the fear and talk about menopause is part of the nonsense of our conventional civilisation.

All in all, what you have got to do with your mate is what the great composers have done with music. You have got to realise that harmony is not something sweet and accessible. Harmony is a resolution after conflict, a rest after strain and effort, a solution after profound differences. Harmony is the culmination of immense unconscious creative processes. It is only when we have the courage to tackle these forces in each other that we become well-mated, strongly-mated, and free. I am married and I feel as free as the air. I am in love and I know that I am loved; I haven't got the slightest dread or fear. I couldn't talk like that if I only had a conventional marriage because, after all, my wife is twenty-six years younger than I am. If I had just a conventional marriage, I would be an old man sipping at a bowl while some young rapscallions would be round pitching their caps at my wife's loveliness.

No, the only road in marriage is to plunge into the discords of marriage, to be forthright and adventurous, always willing to endure ever greater discords for the sake of an ever-growing more beautiful and more intimate harmony. There must be change in a relationship and change is always upsetting. But change is the only source of growth.

THY WILL
BE DONE

CHAPTER FIVE

I want to talk now about how the attitudes of nurses and parents towards toilet-training influences the development of young children to the point where the growth of their personalities may become fixated or stunted in certain ways, because this can have significant effects on the subsequent behaviour of these children when they enter a marriage relationship.

But first we must realise how vital and personal a little child is. He is at the narcissistic stage of development; that is to say, he is in love with himself. He hasn't got much knowledge; he has the knowledge of being loved by others but he hasn't got the knowledge of loving other people. He loves himself and therefore loves with intense affection all his own processes, his breathing, evacuation, and so on. We can't imagine, because we don't enter into the child's imagination, with what intense fervour and eagerness a child regards these processes. And the child and his processes are governed by instinctual drives into which parents very often have little insight. If the child is warm-hearted, for instance, he is good-natured with his excreta and may present it to his parents as a gift. This brings down upon the child the pressure of parental reproof; he becomes aware of the parents' withdrawal

of affection; he is relegated to a state of isolation with
his little love-life all banked up in him, not knowing what
to do with it, not understanding it. So the instinctual life
of the child becomes pent up within itself, creating a state
of anxiety which produces nightmares, sweatings, or even
palpitations and general physical disturbances. But the
parents don't notice it because this invisible thing, this
libido, this life-force, is difficult to understand unless you
put yourself in the child's position. For example, any
woman who sees her husband withdraw from her and go
out and leave her knows what it means to have all her
feelings pent up. Or if a man has his wife's feelings with-
drawn from him, he knows how intense and painful that
experience can be. And yet a grown-up has all the control and development to learn how to deal with these disturbed emotions. A little child's ego is unformed to a
great dgeree and it cannot know how to deal with itself.
It is packed full of these strange emotions leading to anxiety, to a tensed-up state which must be diverted into other
channels.

The first phase in a little child's life is when the little
baby has got no control over his sphincter and therefore
is governed in instinct in bowel movements or urination.
But owing to our type of civilisation, that kind of freedom
cannot exist, cannot remain long unchallenged; so parents do their best to 'educate' their children. The average mother is under the impression that the question of
putting a child on a chamber is a question of precision
by the clock. Many mothers do not realise the evacuatory
process is a biological process and the child can very well
take care of himself in this matter. But there is a myth
existing among some women that a child is going to suffer damage if it is constipated for a day or two. The
child must have regular moments of evacuation and these
are not the child's moments.

These sorts of attitudes towards toilet-training produce
two typical reactions. One appears to be on the surface
a counter-reaction formation. A child builds a kind of
character that gradually defines itself and the line it takes
is this: the child becomes intensely orderly so that it

likes to have everything clean, not only in regard to excretory things but in clothing and the jobs it does; everything connected with its life takes on a pattern of parsimony which in later years becomes one of meanness and obstinacy. Thus, when the initial reaction has disappeared in its simple form, there gradually appears this more complex form of orderliness, obstinacy and parsimony. The person grows up with these three things strongly in the organisation of his or her life. In the case of a woman, the obsession can take the form of insisting on a clean house and demanding that things be orderly and well arranged. The man may insist on excessive order in his business affairs. For example, if he is a student, he will insist on a great orderliness in the arrangement of his notes; he will be very careful to get correct papers drawn up and properly filed. So both a man and a woman extend this orderliness to every aspect of their lives.

Now you might think that because they are so orderly things are satisfactory because orderliness fits in a great deal with the demands of our civilisation. It seems very beautiful and nice; but instead of there being a willingness to co-operate, the moment you make demands on such individuals, you will be amazed at the obstinacy that becomes apparent. This type of person doesn't mind being asked to do something. They don't mind being asked, 'Will you do this or will you do that?' but if there is any attempt, even in the slightest way, to get them to be obedient or to co-operate with anything or anybody, they reveal an immense obstinacy of character. For example, even though they may be generous in their money affairs, they become exceedingly parsimonious.

The other reaction in children to severe toilet-training is quite the opposite. The child develops habits of sloppiness in defiance of his rigid environment and becomes, psychologically speaking, diarroetic rather than constipated. There is often a generosity of spirit with such people, the opposite of parsimony. But this generosity can get them into trouble because, for instance, they constantly buy what they can't afford. When they go out and see something they like, they feel they must have it.

Now if a person has either of these fixations permanently in his make-up, the effect on a marriage relationship can be quite drastic if not understood by the parties to the marriage. And to make things worse, very often two people who want to get married are actually attracted by the similarity of their complexes or fixations.

Imagine a woman being married to a man with these traits. Imagine a man who is absolutely orderly in all his affairs, who makes everything go well, who is an exceedingly fine organiser. At the same time, he hates to pay his bills and hides the fact and doesn't let it be known. He keeps it a secret, if he can. But if you are the grocer waiting for a bill, or the electricity company waiting for a bill, well, heaven help you, because he will delay these bills as much as ever he can. What he is actually doing is constipating. He is carrying into all the affairs of life the constipation rebellion, where he constipated himself as a little infant, in revulsion against his mother's insistent rigidity. Although he is orderly, although he has become obedient to his parents or his nurse to the extent that he is clean, obsessively clean, in regard to giving things he is just parsimonious.

I know women who have longed for a spring coat or a spring dress, and they have gone window-shopping and picked out all the little frocks they would like and the coats they would like and the hats they would like. But try to get their husbands to pay and they will present a dozen different reasons why they shouldn't. And in reality, they don't want to pay for it. They have carried this constipated act so profoundly into their character that it is with the greatest pain that they finally surrender. In some instances, men will wait until they are taken to court, until the county court has issued a summons against them, before they will finally pay. As I say, that is bad enough, but when the wife seeks to get an understanding with such a man there is an obstinacy that is quite unbelievable. He puts forward rationalisations as to why he should do this and why she should do that.

But the thing is equally tragic if the woman has such

a fixation. For example, many men can't even go into a room in their own home without putting their slippers on. The room must be kept so clean and so tidy by the over-tidying wife, the clean wife, that home becomes a very nasty place. They can stretch their legs in any place except their own drawing room or dining room. If they happen to make little mistakes at table as to how they carve the meat or how they eat the meat, then God help them, for the wife will let them know, not necessarily with open rows but with that superior disdain that belongs to superior people! And these wives carry this superiority right through household work, and they make the men ashamed if they don't shave, ashamed if their shoes aren't polished, ashamed—in other words—if they aren't clean in every way. Such women openly express great disgust of untidy men; let a man go two days without a shave with one of these women, and they regard it as a major crime against mankind.

On top of this, this type of character formation absorbs so much psychic energy in fixated behaviour that very often the wife who is most orderly and efficient and clean and stubborn is incapable of any vital adult physical feminine sexuality. The drain-off of energy to the 'hang-up' in her personality is so profound that the whole of the physical side of sex and the mental side of sex can be utterly impoverished, so that a man feels doubts whether his wife loves him because they can never have the joy of orgasm, the joy of abandoned sex relations.

On the other hand, it can act the other way round, so that the man has got an immense capacity for organising, an immense capacity for cleanliness; but when it comes to love-making, he is incapable of it, for he is fixated at the narcissistic stage of love, that is to say, the first stage of evolution of personality where the child explores the zones of its own body, the zones of its own mind, expanding inwardly to know itself. It has not yet got to know the non-self, the objective world; it has no love to give yet to the objective world. Because a person fixated at this stage of development is closed in on himself or herself, in the marriage situation when quarrels occur, things

are much more difficult. Instead of having the outgoing
affection that comes from true heterosexual growth—
where the man loves his woman and feels with her and
for her, and where a woman feel with and loves her man
—the husband and the wife are set opposite each other in
the same household and quarrel over the same things,
and are inaccessible to one another spiritually. Although
they are talking words, although they are arguing with
each other, there is no warmth, there is no illumination,
for they are not seeking each other at all unconsciously.
They are saying, 'My will be done.' And the other person
is saying equally, 'My will be done.' The situation is
worse if side by side with that there is an impoverish-
ment of the sexual life. The man may make love to his
wife in vain because she is not responsive, she can give
no return; equally, the man may be unresponsive and, in
some instances, both may be, because they are bottled up
in this way, auto-erotically. Each of them has not yet lost
his own life in order to find each other's. They have not
discovered the meaning of the saying, 'He who would find
his own life must lose it.' They haven't come to that de-
parture of the self into the outer world, which allows love
to flow forth and bind and cement their spirits and minds
together. There is not available the binding force that
makes a marriage, the gracious intimacy that grows and
grows when you talk frankly soul to soul with somebody
you love. When this situation arises, because the rivers
of life have not flowed forth, they are still flowing and
accumulating in the psyche begetting conditions of intense hyper-sensitive anxiety, so that the two people become immensely irritable with each other. They quarrel
readily and frequently because they are enraged against
each other, each looking upon the other as the enemy of
freedom and a hindrance to self-expression. But, unfortunately in all of this, the real problem remains undiscov-
ered. This is the tragedy of human life: they know not
what they do. It is not that they are aware of all this,
it is that they are unaware. Both secretly feel starved:
disillusionment sets in. Instead of accepting the burden
of marriage, instead of accepting each other, and ac-

cepting all the limits and all the good, and all the ills
that are in each other, one or the other begins a private campaign with himself about the other mate;
and sooner or later they both have their private cam-
paigns going. In this first phase they don't gossip to
anybody else. They are horrified: they have gone into marriage thinking how wonderful it is, and how
splendid it is, how magnificent it is, and they have stum-
bled across this extraordinary confusion and lack of fulfilment. Now the man asks himself: 'Does my woman
love me? Wouldn't she be excited by me, if she loved me?
Couldn't I quicken her, if she loved me?' And the woman herself feels isolated: 'Is this all that marriage is? I
thought it was going to be wonderful. My husband doesn't
want to caress me; he has no interest in me.' There begins a spiritual assassination within the home which destroys marriages, an egotistical, narcissistic tribunal in
which you bring your mate up before judgement, but
don't say a word. You go to bed at night and put your
arms round each other in utmost deceit, each afraid to
discuss his or her own private tragedy with the other.
Shakepeare's magnificent lines go unheeded: 'Love is not
love which alters when it alteration finds, or bends with
the remover to remove; O, no! it is an ever-fixed mark,
that looks at tempests and is never shaken.'

Instead of extending themselves into the outer world,
people with such fixations regress back into themselves
causing what we in psycho-analysis call 'affectivity.' That
is to say, this energy, instead of discharging outwardly
by forming fruitful relationships, comes back and is absorbed by the circulatory system of the body and the secretory system of the body and puts the individual into a
state of dis-ease. The beginning of all disease is a state
of dis-ease. For this state of affectivity is a state that is
accompanied by a state of anxiety and tension that cannot be endured unless it is converted; and primary conversion is into the secretory and circulatory systems, producing all sorts of disturbances within the body. And then
begins the hysterical conversion where the classical symptoms occur which help the analyst to diagnose according

to his training and insight; but unless he is aware of the fundamental background that lies behind the whole business he may be bewildered, because sometimes a patient can exhibit many syndromes as the years go on. For the illness that first began just as a functional change can by persistence be carried further. And even where infection is involved, the micro-organisms are more damaging to a body which is psychosomatic charged in this manner. And medicine itself is coming more and more to understand this psychosomatic aspect of things.

And when it comes to helping a marriage like this, whether it be a doctor, psychologist, or clergyman who is attempting to help, it is important to know what kind of complex gave rise to the problem in the first place.

I hope I have done enough to show that if two people find themselves gripped by the complex I am revealing to you, they at least should try to solve it by learning to talk to each other. If in discussing your childhood you become aware of the factors which helped make you what you are, you are already easing the problem: confession is good for the soul. You learn to tell your partner, and this in turn illumines their own childhood experiences. In this way, the early instinctual life mysteriously and beautifully merges into the ego and begins cementing the two people together. This ego, when fully filled out in this manner, is able to withstand enormous pressures from society. The human mind is not like a ramrod or a concrete pole, it is like a beautifully designed yacht that can take every pressure of wind and storm; with skillful sailing, the yacht won't capsise. Neither does the mind. The breaking point of the mind is far far beyond what people think it is; and thousands of breakdowns could be saved if people would learn that the mind is like a yacht dancing along amid impulses, ideas, and feelings, which, all the while, maintains a direction, something central and spiritual in man that coheres all these things and brings them into unity.

When two people talk to each other in this manner, instead of mutual judgement you get mutual growth. And when you have thus refreshed each other you go out into society bringing not bitterness and rancour as before but beauty, truth, and hope. Without knowing it, you are cohering society; you are creating the mystery of fellowship. Fellowship is the capacity of interflow between all persons, the capacity to let down the drawbridge of our ego and go forth meeting one another in creative love! The very thing that you misuse by keeping it within the intimacy of your soul, when properly used, heals not only your own marriage but helps to heal others as well.

THE LION
AND
THE LAMB

CHAPTER SIX

A little boy and a little girl in the course of their development from one to three really cover again the five hundred million years of the evolution of man. In those years, the child makes rapid growth in which he passes through vast changes that are not observable except by people trained to observe or by people with sufficient sympathy to understand. This rapid growth includes the blossoming forth of certain tendencies which if they develop normally are very useful in later life. Now it sometimes happens that these tendencies, which everyone has to some extent, become exaggerated or fixated at the childish level because something prevents their normal development, and when this happens the results in later life can be very sad. Here I want to talk about two of these tendencies or instincts, the tendency to aggression which Freud called sadism and the tendency of self-punishment which he called masochism. You could say that aggression is the male instinct, but of course there is no such thing as a complete male and a complete female; everyone has a greater or lesser proportion of both male and female in them. One of the ways this proportion is determined is by the way in which the child successfully gets through

the aggression and self-punishment phase of development
which begins at about three years of age.

What is the nature of these instincts? The masochistic
and sadistic instincts are related to the biological struggle
of life not only with man but with all living creatures.
Aggression is that energy in an animal that is expressed
in rage. When an animal is full of rage he will attack
and if he can, destroy his enemy ruthlessly. And if you
see two primitive animals fighting one another, you will
see the sadistic instinct laid bare for your beholding where
there seems to be no referee, nobody to step in and say,
'Wait, stop, let's try to understand,' and the creatures
usually fight until one is completely defeated and flees
in terror or one or the other dies or the two of them die.
But the point I want you to notice is the intense amount
of energy in that rage. If one could transfer it from rage
to steam power or electric power, you could do an immense amount of work with it. As the young child grows,
this aggressive instinct or potential also grows within
him.

Side by side with this, there grows the instinct of self-
punishment or tendency towards passivity, if you want
to put it that way. It is an odd instinct and difficult to
understand. It is an instinct where a creature turns on
itself and may even go so far as to destroy itself. Now
anyone with little children who has his eyes open will
realise that, in the main, girls in their development have
a passive trend and boys have an aggressive trend. You
will notice your little boy cruel towards worms which he
will cut in two, cruel towards cats, cruel towards animals.
Some parents are very surprised to see how ruthless their
innocent little child can be, enjoying catching flies and
putting them into a spider's web and enjoying seeing
them attacked and eaten, and so on. In its gross form
this instinct has puzzled many people.

The biologist will tell you that this aggression has
helped animals to preserve themselves in the struggle of
life. It has made them more swift, more powerful, more
courageous, for a creature under the impetus of the aggressive instinct has immense courage.

Equally, self-punishment or passivity is important in the struggle for existence, although this instinct is a little more difficult to understand. It is a form of enjoyment of self. You can see this when a child has a cut or a wound: it will pick it. It does it because it gets a special psychological pleasure out of those things, not just pleasure related to physical pain, but a psychological pleasure.

Now, a lot of learning with regard to these two instincts takes place in the child between the ages of five and twelve when the physical sexual life seems to go into a sort of latency. And this learning is very important in the formation of character.

In the boy some of his sadism becomes strength of character, lets him study hard at his work, lets him attack problems, and it gives him energy. With a girl, her masochism allows her to endure, to nurse the sick, to carry a child through a nine-month pregnancy, and to do the many tedious chores involved in the rearing of a family. As well as this, taken together in the evolution of man, the two instincts blend in later life and produce sympathy. The aggressive character cannot understand until it meets aggression turned on itself and thereby suffers; the self-punishing character learns by seeing the effect of the instinct in others. Anyway, when these two instincts blend together, they are of the highest value in producing very fine types of people, full of tenderness and strength and sympathy.

Now I want to show the kind of thing that happens in a marriage if the aggression and self-punishment instincts have not developed in the normal way.

Let me take an instance of this. I will take an unusual instance where a husband and a wife perhaps were first drawn together because of this very thing. The husband was fixated at the childhood phase of the self-punishment; psychologically he was only around four years old, although when I saw him he was over forty and a man of brilliant attainment, a man who had already done great work in the world and was an expert at his work in his own right. The wife was a sadist. In other words, they were both stuck psychologically at the age of four of five

and had grown up no more than that. Although their
bodies had grown up and they had become physically sexual and physically differentiated, they were fundamentally
governed by the secret 'hang-up' within their two souls.
The result was that the woman, who was herself an educated woman, a woman of ability and a woman of charm,
became authoritarian. She was bossy in a quiet kind of
way, not loud-mouthed or loud-spoken, but she dominated
her husband in every possible way. When people were in
the house she would say, 'I want you to bring that, dear.'
Not 'Will you bring it?' but 'I want you to bring that,
dear.' And because he was fixated at the self-punishment
stage, the opposite, she was getting pleasure in being cruel
with him and he was getting pleasure in being tortured.
Can you see what I mean? Unconsciously, not consciously
at all, he wished to be miserable; and her pleasure in life
was to be fundamentally cocky and bossy. Now although
they started out well and intended a good marriage, and
had a lovely prior life several months before marriage,
that marriage gradually disintegrated.

I was called in when that marriage was on the rocks.
The man himself, although he was able and acknowledged,
had superiors over him in his particular job. He hadn't
got many but he had got two or three superiors. And because he was self-punishing, he unconsciously tried to get
himself into trouble, and did things that could only bring
him into trouble, such as arranging to do some work in-
volving a team of people and not being there when the
team turned up to make the piece of work necessary. And
unconsciously, although he was shocked when he found
that he didn't go there, this is precisely what he wanted.
It is hard to understand how someone could behave this
way but, in fact, he wanted to be punished, he wanted to
be isolated, he wanted to be cast out. Therefore, not only
did he have this sort of relationship with his wife, but he
was self-punishing or passive with any superior, any person who talked with authority. They only had to talk with
an authoritative voice and he became subservient. He
couldn't stand up for himself, he couldn't argue his case.
He let everything go by default. But there was a deeper

tragedy; because he had become fundamentally passive and his wife had become fundamentally sadistic or aggressive, their sexual life was absolutely upset. For she couldn't get any sexual pleasure if she was in the inferior position sexually; she could only get sexual pleasure if she was in the superior position. Only then was she capable of sexual orgasm. And therefore many and many a time her sex relations were a tragedy. Although it started out beautifully and was full of beautiful promise and beautiful fulfillment, she was incapable of that feminine response by which a woman alone can get orgastic pleasure. She was unable to maintain the passive position in which radiant ecstasy would flow through her. She was unable to hold that because of this drive that was making her manlike. It later on affected her hormones and her breasts began to get smaller although there was no physical reason for this. However, there certainly were psychological reasons.

When they separated after several attempts to unite, the interesting thing is that she wrote letters to him and every letter she sent him was cruel. It wasn't apparent, but if you read sentence by sentence she was doing all she could to make him suffer anguish. He wanted her back, yet every sentence of hers was hostile. 'I will write to you now and again, but I will only give you commonplace details.' In every sentence that woman wrote, the unconscious, assertive hostility, the unconscious rage, was burning. And the husband, when he read these letters, felt completely suicidal, partly because it shattered him and partly because he wanted to enjoy the agony and the pain of it.

This self-punishment is a most difficult thing to understand. You can see it in some of the saints who lay on beds made of nails, thinking in some way that they were helping their communion with God. But in the case of such mystics, modern psychology can distinguish between the spiritual aspect of their lives and the abnormal aspect where they thought they gave pleasure to God if they lay on nails. They got pleasure because they enjoyed the pain. Now there is an insidious aspect to this problem. Sometimes you can obviously see that the persons in question got themselves into situations of physical pain. But it is far more subtle when the spirit or imagination of the person, the whole soul tends towards this thing. It makes the man feminine instead of masculine, and makes the woman masculine instead of feminine. And of course the reverse can take place where an absolute brute of a man allies himsef with a woman who is passive and possibly very cultured. He spends his life torturing that woman and gets his pleasure in torturing her, not in loving her in any way. But oddly enough, if she is the self-punishing type, she gets her pleasure in being tortured. Although you might not believe it, she will even go out of her way to prevent any attempt to expose this thing and bring it to conscious knowledge. Instead of being grateful for such help, she will be the opposite. I have sample proof of this. When I press this point with such ladies, the most refined of them become abusive. I have had pillows thrown at me more than a dozen times by women you think couldn't even say a naughty word. But when I investigated the situation and got the other side of their personality, they let me know it without any trouble. And they used language you wouldn't find in Billingsgate, although consciously they had no capacity for it and were refined people and cultured people. Now you may find this strange, and you may say that you don't believe it. But if you happen to go to places where these instincts in their perversity are laid open, such as in a mental hospital, you will have no doubt about it. For you will see what happens when the thing develops into the ultimate tragedy of mental breakdown.

This then is an instance of where a woman is over-feminised and the man over-masculined. Neither of them gives each other the rapture of sex. For the man who is brutal in his sexuality cannot tenderly woo a woman, and a woman, unless she is tenderly and delicately wooed in her body and her spirit, cannot possibly come to the yearning of sexual delight. An American lady told me that there were no frigid women, there were only clumsy men. Now it is not necessarily true, but she had a point. For if a man has got too much sadism in his character, he is so anxious, even on the physical side, to proceed from desire to action that he has not the slightest idea that the body of woman is a musical harp to be delicately awakened and to be delicately prepared. So in this kind of marriage you have the tragic fact that the man himself only gets the most arrogant, primitive form of sexual utterance, and the woman often breaks down through sexual starvation because they have not had any proper orgastic pleasure, even after years of marriage.

We must all be both male and female, otherwise there is no hope of understanding the nature and needs of our partners. At the same time, our maleness or femaleness must be the mature kind. If they are the childish forms of aggression and self-punishment, we become too self-centered to allow a knowledge and understanding of others to enter us and become the sympathetic element in our personalities.

RE-
MEMBRANCE
OF
THINGS PAST

CHAPTER SEVEN

Why is it that so many marriages that start off with such hope, that start off with such vision, that start off with such eagerness, end after a few years rather grimly or dimly or commonplace? I have watched the romance with which many people came into marriage, and I have seen it fade away, and the faces of the people become harder, more set, more bitter. There certainly was not the high magic that they imagined.

Now was the high magic a delusion? When they went into marriage full of vision, was that vision a delusion? And if it is not a delusion, can we give any account as to why marriage fails?

Now I want to talk about one of the reasons why many marriages become so stale. It has to do with what Freud called the 'Oedipus' phase of growing-up, and what happens if people get stuck in this phase and do not get through it successfully.

When they are growing up, boys and girls learn how to be men and women by imitating their parents. They sometimes do this so well that the little boy may come to think of himself as his father's rival in a bid for the mother's affection, and the little girl may come to see her mother as her rival in a bid for the father's affection. Freud called this situation the 'Oedipus complex' after the legendary Greek hero who unwittingly killed his father and married his own mother. In normal development, this is really just a stage in the expanding awareness of the growing child when he learns about the differences between men and women and begins to adopt his own individual pattern of reaction to each of the sexes. Unfortunately, the atmosphere in some homes prevents this stage of development from going very smoothly and what should be a quick and easy progression in development becomes a traumatic experience and the cause of a permanent 'hang-up' or 'complex' in the personality.

How does this happen? As I said, children imitate their parents. They try to be as strong and as brave and as lovely as they think their parents are. The daughter tries to be like her mother in all her glory and the boy tries to be like his father in all his glory. This can go so far that the little boy passionately loves his mother and the little girl passionately loves her father and they become rivals of the parent of the same sex.

Now in a true home this leads to intense jealousy. If brothers and sisters are born, the same secondary sexual attraction arises, the sisters being more careful of the brothers than they are of their own sisters, and so on. If we had a true type of education in the home and a true type of understanding, these jealousies would be allowed quite adequate expression, but we are such hypocrites in our Christian civilisation that we imagine our homes are peaceful, loving, kind, holy places; and by holy I mean no disorder, no anger, no hate, no jealousy, no envy. This is just a complete lie and it is time that Christians got to it and saw that it is a lie.

Now in order to keep the lie up this is what parents do: whenever they see any excess of jealousy, any excess of anger, any excess of exhibitionism, or peeping, or anything else, they squash it. In other words they punish what they don't want to take place. So the order in a lot of so-called Christian homes is not the result of harmony but of suppression.

For example, if my little boy wants to turn on the electric fire, I tell him no. If I find him turning it on I smack him. He will then put the fire on any time I am not there because he hasn't been defeated. But if I come in two or three days after and still find him putting on the fire and give him a very thorough thrashing and shout at him, a change takes place within that little boy. He never tries any more to turn on the fire. Why? Because he has made me his inward, harsh conscience. This is not the true conscience that the theologians declare is the voice of God within the soul, but my harsh conscience. My son, in order to accommodate to my environment and in dread of my punishment, alters himself so that somebody inside of him now watches himself, and the other little mischievous boy that is still wanting to turn on the fire is pushed right out into the unconscious mind. He no longer consciously wants to turn on the fire, but unconsciously he does. So there is a mental conflict set up that he is unaware of, a conflict in which all these desires of his are living in rebellion against me, but because he is terrified of me he suppresses his real self.

Now if that takes place when a little boy wants to do a mischievous thing like that, when he really wants to assert himself he is more than ever crushed. Or if a little girl wants to show off the way big girls do, she is laughed at and kept down. So in our Christian homes we never get to know this hidden conflict, we never encounter our children's passions, we never live close to the intense, immense energy of child life. We use these punishments as very clever ways of casting childhood out of the heart of children into the unconscious deep, and the child is left with an unknown self struggling to express itself. But if you block a river going its ordinary course, that river will gather force and find a new path, and if you block that, then it seeks a new path, and if you block that, again it seeks a new path. And in a similar way, the child strives to bring up all these outcast forces into some kind of expression, but it will not now be a straightforward, open action as he wanted it to be. Instead of our child being a straightforward, honest little man, or a straightforward, honest little woman, we have taught them not to be honest, we have taught them to be immensely furtive. Our little children learn a furtiveness beyond our belief, and they carry out their dreams in ways that they don't even know themselves. Conscious control is lost sight of and the energy is handed over to unconsciousness.

Now that is bad enough when it comes to things like wanting to light the fire, but when it comes to a son desiring his mother, or a boy desiring his sister, or a daughter desiring her daddy, or a sister yearning for her brother, these are such terrible desires, according to our bankrupt, critical civilisation, that we can't tolerate such feelings in our children and whenever they appear we are filled with horror. Instead of allowing the home to be the place where a child can learn control by conscious suffering, instead of reasoning with the child, instead of caring for the child, instead of going with the child step by step and day by day with its inner life, we are so busy with our getting and our spending and our business and our social life, and our friends and ourselves, that we've got no time to be genuine parents. We are not genuine parents and as a result, and just as a rubber can rub off everything we don't want on a page, we rub out of the conscious mind anything we don't like in our children. They then look nice and clean, exactly as you want them to be, but underneath are the flaming forces of unfulfilled wishes. And what is the result? The result is that the personality never resolves all these conflicting forces and it never brings them to a final union and a final synthesis in the personality, and the personality is left split underneath and unconsciously.

And when some girls have not only got a father but two or three brothers whom they love, and a boy has not only his mother but two or three sisters whom he loves, the task of bringing these into one great river of life is a tremendous one which few people achieve.

Apart from suppressing the feelings of our children, there are other ways in which we prevent them from developing. Suppose that a boy has been intensely in love with his mother who, instead of attending to him, has fairly well ignored him. This takes place particularly in the upper classes where a woman will go away on holidays and leave her little child in the hands of nurses or 'au pairs' who are strangers to the child. The little boy may have an intense ache of love for his mother. But suddenly the mother is rubbed out, she suddenly disappears. Try and think of that! If you had a girl you were in love with or a man you were in love with and they suddenly disappeared for a year's holiday without telling you, what would you feel like? If you had a lover and he just left you all packed with pain and unfulfilled love, how would you feel? But we go away from our little children who even at the age of three months are aware of this love and ache to be loved, but we don't care a button. We go off like that for half a day, or a day, or a week, or two weeks, and the little child is left with his pent-up love for an object that does not answer his love. A child needs love more than he needs the mother breast. This is a fact. He needs the mother-love and the father-love more than he needs his material supports and it is more essential to his soul.

But parents who go off and leave children like this have no understanding of how delicate a thing the growth of emotion in a child is. And when these things happen to a child his emotions become all 'bottled up' and don't really become integrated into his personality, and he develops an 'Oedipus complex,' which affects all his subsequent behaviour. For example, when someone with an Oedipus complex arrives at the adolescent period he may fall in love with a girl who is somewhat older than himself and usually a very fine type of girl, a type of girl who will be a true mother to him, who can take care of him. The whole of his secret, furtive, unknown love for the mother is projected onto her because part of himself remembers her when she was younger. He can very easily enter into an intimate sex relation with her, win her love, and draw her out and make her helpless in his keeping, but he cannot give the totality of his unconscious feelings to her because she only represents to him his mother at a particular period of her life. So what happens is this: after he has had that relationship with a girl who is, say, in her thirties or forties, he suddenly and unaccountably falls in love with a girl who is much younger and more beautiful. He is falling in love with the mother that he knew when she was young and he lay in her arms and gazed up into her wonderful face and beheld her beauty, beheld her loveliness. And he is amazed at the rich affection that he is able to give to this woman. There surges up in him unbelievable tenderness, unbelievable audacity of love, unbelievable abandon of love because the cast-out spirit that his parents compelled him to repress in his early days is now coming forward into the situation.

Now suppose the person he falls in love with is also married, and this frequently occurs. The other mate in the relationship is then involved in unbelievable anguish of soul because up to that time he thought he had his mate for himself, and now he must accommodate himself to the idea that he must share his mate with somebody else. The woman has imagined that her husband was adequately satisfied. But she, like the man, is not adequately satisfied because she also is seeking her daddy through this new lover. They rationalise it in a most amazing way by putting forward new theories of sex relationship, the dawn of a new age, the coming of a new freedom and sophistication. But the proof of it is the damage that is done to the human beings involved. If a man has three or four such relationships, and smashes three or four other marriages, well that's the price that is being paid for a rigid up-bringing. If then, such a person falls in love with a girl he can marry, that girl receives whatever libido he can give, the libido being the life force, the love force given to the marriage. Now the marriage looks excellent, the two people are enamoured of each other, they care very much for each other, and all seems well. You wonder what is happening a few years afterwards when things are not well? Let me illustrate what is taking place. The girl has only been able to give a part of her love to her lover, for some of it is with her father, deep down in the secret heart at the age of one to four, a deep, warm love burning there. Likewise the boy, the little son, can't give his total love to his wife although he's been in love with her.

What then? For a time their love is adequate because the people have never had such love, they've never had such intimacy, they've never had such beauty before, and everything seems well. But after a while another girl comes into the boy's life and the wife can't help noticing that his eyes light up when that girl comes into the room; she can't help noticing he's musing, day-dreaming. Or the same with the girl: a husband can't help noticing how quickened a girl is, that she blushes when a certain man comes into her presence. In a very short time an affair develops, two people are drawn together, they hardly know how, by deep, unconscious forces that are lying in the soul, and they start to talk intimacies to each other, usually general intimacies, not fundamental intimacies, but this is the beginning of a very important intimacy, and a betrayal.

And so an unresolved 'Oedipus complex'—the hidden unconscious store of love-energy—becomes the stimulus for infidelity.

Now you can imagine therefore that this is the actual situation with most married people today, and not only married people but unmarried people. You have got on the surface a love-force that you've openly vowed to in civilisation: in our civilisation it is the vow of marriage, and you wear the ring as proof of your conjunction with one another. But deep underneath are streams unknown to yourself, libidinal streams that are running like underground rivers, compelling you to link up with this person and link up with that person rather than meet the tragedy of the situation. The old-fashioned idea that you take each other '... for better for worse, for richer for poorer, in sickness and in health, to love and to cherish, till death us do part,' is an absolutely correct promise to the Oedipus situation, but we don't do it. We don't remain loyal to each other. A woman goes off and lives her other life or a man goes off and lives his other life, instead of confronting their mate in a fight to bring this suppressed love-energy to the surface. For love is the one essential thing, it is the one thing that mustn't be broken, not even if you don't get it all your life. If you've made your bond to your woman or your man, it doesn't matter what she does in waywardness, or what he does in waywardness; unless one of you maintains this unbreakable truth of holy marriage, there is no union between men and women that will not smash under the vicissitudes of life. But if one of the people will hold during that agony, if one will hold right to the end, endure to the end, the odds are that your husband or your wife in the end will come home to you, and come home to you with the full, rich splendour of their whole love-energy.

But I say that men and women in this generation are starved of this. There are very few genuine, fundamental, joyous marriages held together by the unbreakable bond of holy love.

Now I agree that some marriages break up because the people didn't love at the first. Such marriages, in my judgement, do not count, for if God has not joined you together in my opinion then you are not joined together. Those whom God hath joined together let no man put asunder, but if you have married for a convenience, or if you have married for any trickery, such a marriage will not hold unless you discover a deeper love in which you can be redeemed.

A true marriage should be a relationship of spiritual fellowship that includes body, mind, and spirit in union. Although that is a perfection to be aimed at, it is not a perfection in the skies, a receding object that one never reaches, but an ideal to be achieved within the struggle of marriage. I don't think marriage is worth a button unless it is a marriage where the two people can gradually disclose themselves to each other, revealing not only the window-dressing that people show to one another when they are courting, but also the things that arise when they've got to live day by day with each other in all the vicissitudes and difficulties of living.

And in our sophisticated modern society, people who are not prepared to put this effort into marriage make all sorts of excuses for their behaviour. They say the present system of social organisation, of family relations and sex relation isn't right and that this experience in them is due to their high evolution: 'I'm a finer type than the average person, I'm an evolution sport, I belong to a higher order and in me is a new age.' Now, I'm not denying that that could be possible, that another form of marriage or another form of relationship could emerge. I do not know. But I'm certain of one thing, if the new age is going to come with another form of marriage, it must go through the open gate of spiritual monogamy. Now that seems an utter contradiction, but the new age, if it comes, if it is going to allow any liberty, can only allow liberty if it has grown out of the perfect love of the perfect married lovers, who have given their total love-energy to their husband or their wife, and this is one of the rarest things in modern civilisation. Now you may say this is a pessimistic conclusion, a 'hard thing' that I say, but it is not. It is an utterly optimistic conclusion. It is the conclusion that only love, rich, full, and abandoned, has any power in life, and no one is united to anybody unless the whole joy of their being in love is poured out onto the other person. And what I have said does not tie us to conventional forms of marriage just because they are blessed at this time or any other time, for if in God's mercy any new vision of marriage comes, if in God's light new orders shall appear, without a doubt that new order will come, without a doubt it will be born because it is in the mind of God and is in his keeping. But nobody can step into that realm of marriage, no one is going to step into that new order, if it is going to come, unless you step into it with all your deep, fundamental love-energy at the service of such a marriage, until you are full of free love in the spiritual sense, that is, free from a longing for father, mother, brother, or sister. Until you are freed from that you are not safe.

A LIGHT WITHIN

CHAPTER EIGHT

Now I want to talk here about the development of a moral sense in people and how this can go wrong. Freud called this aspect of personality the 'super-ego,' by which he meant the faculty which overlooks or judges the behaviour of the rest of the personality.

I want to clarify this super-ego or moral sense so that we can have a hint as to its nature. When a child is first born, the influence of the parents is predominant and very powerful, for the parents not only give their influence as father and mother but they give their influence as members of the community at a certain cultural level and at a certain social level. According to the group into which a child is born, the parents are not merely the voices of authority, they are the voices of value, of general value. The significance of this aspect of the role of parents is underlined by the well-known examples of the 'wolf-child' or the 'gazelle-child.' In these cases the child was taken away as a baby and brought up by an animal. These children did not in any way receive a full human inheritance. Although they had the genetic intelligence of humanity, they could never become like normal human children. So that it is not enough to have the genetic inheritance which comes biologically to the child, you must have the essential

environment which belongs to civilised humanity. However, even given this, depending on the nature of the environment and how he copes with it, the child can develop
or not develop in quite different ways and this is particularly true in the development of a moral sense in people.

During the early years of a child's development, there
is no moral sense. At this stage his guide is always the
external voice of the parents or of parent substitutes such
as aunties, cousins, or servants—any adults who impinge
on the child and demand its attention. Now it is important
to remember that the child and his relationships with others are intensely personal, and because of this the child
learns the norms and values of the adults with whom he as-
sociates. The next stage is when he has learned these values
so that he follows them even when there is no one around.
The parental influence he has learned becomes his moral
sense. He internalises the strictures of his parents and
his moral sense criticises him exactly like mummy and
daddy criticised the child, exactly like the teachers and
the aunties criticised the child. So that there is now existing in the child a division of its personality in which there
is a constant watch held on the child's behaviour from
within. And as a boy identifies himself with the daddy
and the daddy substitutes, and the girl with the mummy
and the mummy substitutes, more and more of this super-
ego or moral sense is built up. Where there is a proper
development of the moral sense, this stage also passes
away and instead of the super-ego being like the voice of
the parents speaking with authority like giants within the
personality, the person becomes interested more in what
is just and what is loving and what is righteous and what
is true. In other words, instead of having parents as authorities internalised, we have ethical principles involved.
So, whenever there is a true development of the personality, control passes away from harsh or strict internalised
parent demands, it passes away from personal demands as
such, to principles of truth, to principles of goodness, to
principles of beauty. And so there develops in man an
inner light, a beacon to guide him. Various names have
been given to this because all men, especially mystics, from

the beginning of time have noticed this thing. Jesus said: 'The kingdom of Heaven is within you.' He held that within every person there is a sense of right and truth which isn't only his inner light and guide to behaviour but is in fact related to a kingdom of truth and spiritual beauty. At the very centre of personality is this reality; and only when you live according to this kingdom within you do you conform to beauty, do you grow up, do you become a capable adult person and a person who sees things in terms of truth and beauty and love, not only caring for yourself individually, but equally caring for your wife, your husband, or your children; and not only for them but for all humanity including your bitterest enemies. So your conduct gradually conforms not to the demands of the original parents, but to a light within you, an illumination coming to you gradually. And it comes very richly in late adolescence, where people become very susceptible, very sensitive, very delicate in their perception of beauty, in their perception of love, in their perception of duty. And I suggest that what is missing in the normal Freudian analysis of growth is this passing over from authoritative rule of a personal God—if you like in the sense of the personal father and mother and their substitutes—to personal principles and values. So that a person who has a well-developed superego or moral sense coming to the point of this development gradually passes away from the sense of being ruled by tyrant gods or tyrant authorities within himself to being guided by a light within him to which he wishes to submit. He wants to be that fine, kind person, and is not happy if he is not that sort of person. And the demand is no longer oppressive, no longer obsessive, no longer urgently guilty. That sense of intense guilt and shame passes away. And it is not a negative question of being punished, and trying to keep out of punishment; it is a positive assertion of a new type of life, that if we follow this life then we will be happy in the home—the husband, the wife and the children. And this serenity will even affect some of the people next door, and the people next door to them, and so on throughout your sphere of influence. Some people express this condition in religious terms saying they have arrived back at the original conception of a divine father guiding them and helping them. Some call it conscience. Others, deep thinkers and mystics and philosophers like Kant, for example, say they are governed by a categorical imperative; that there is something in the human soul which makes a man not like unto himself so much as like unto everybody else. He wouldn't do a thing, Kant said, if it hurt anybody. So act that your act will hurt nobody, so that your act will be true to all humanity as well as to yourself. Because man has got that inherent desire of categorical imperative, Kant said, this must be a divine light in the soul of man; because it comes to all souls sooner or later, this inner light, this truth; and they have a sense of guilt if they turn away from it, a sense of shadow. You might be surprised that I mention Jesus above. People think I do this because I am a Christian. Well, when they do that, they completely misunderstand the kind of person I am. I did not come to the Christian faith because I was brought up in it. Although I was brought up in it I renounced it at quite an early age and became completely agnostic about it. But I found out something in my searches which led me again to a religious point of view. I found out that Jesus has got profound things to say about the healing of the spirit.

Now let me give you a simple tip. At first you will think there is nothing in it, unless you ponder on it. On one occasion Jesus said, 'The Kingdom of Heaven is within you.' Now I suggest that if you try to understand that, and you look inside yourself as I have tried to, you will be completely bewildered because all you get is a blank and a darkness or, at least, an immense vacantness. But I suggest that it is as if you put your eyes onto the horizon when you are waiting for a ship. And you know this ship is coming in, and yet your sight doesn't take the ship in at all because it is not yet within sight. But if you know that the ship is coming and concentrate on the horizon, sooner or later it will appear. That is how it comes, very vague at first, only gradually defining itself. In the same way, David the psalmist said, 'Be still and know that I am God.'

I suggest that if you do gaze within yourself, and relax

and don't try to understand anything, after you have done that for a few days, the first thing you are aware of seems quite intangible but is utterly real. What you are aware of is a quiet sense of inner peace and relaxation which you never knew before. Through nothing else but this intent gazing in and seeing nothing and getting no apparent answer, as if you are looking at shadows, you will be amazed that there comes to you a most profound quiet and inner balance.

Then there comes a further development. With this inner peace, instead of going out and fighting with people and getting excited and working yourself up, you find you can be absolutely quiet.

Gradually the other people begin to sense that there is a quality in you that brings them peace. They feel, when they are talking to you, as if all the fret and trouble and all the conflict in their hearts starts to gently pass away like a storm ending on the sea. They are aware that in your presence they can no longer engage in the mood that they had before. What has actually happened is that without knowing it the mood of the world has passed away and another mood of healing and quietness and love has come in them. The people are learning a containment and a restfulness of heart that they have never known.

I believe that in that peace, if it were experimented in, there would be an immense realm of healing that is hidden from us today. As you know, the majority of psychoanalysts have no interest in religion. They are so fascinated with their science that they don't press beyond it. I press beyond it because I have learned from Jesus and David that the western world has lost an immense amount of knowledge. It is far more priceless than all the scientific knowledge we have got today because it feeds the heart and the soul, while the other only feeds the senses and the intellect.

But the development of this inner light in people doesn't always go well because some parents don't understand the process. Many parents obtain obedience from children through punishment. When a child does what they think is naughty they say, 'Stop that!,' 'Don't do that!' And so the child gets a negative education in punishments in the main. The parents sometimes show a certain amount of anger, even if they don't intend it; they show anger on their face, and they show arrogance on their face. Naturally children have a tendency to withdraw from parents when they frighten them like that. And that sort of child gradually withdraws some of its love which would naturally flow out in a loving home, but which cannot come out if there is too much strictness. If the child is treated like this the type of moral sense it learns, the type of parent strictures which it internalises will be based on fear. And the child is then in the position that it is not only threatened when the parents are present, but the threats which have been given to the child in the end make him obedient even when the parents are not present. So that, because he has been smacked several times, he won't go near the fire even when he is alone. He won't go near the electric switch when he is alone, because he has been smacked and he has been told not to. In the main, mothers are very quick to smack a child because it is the quickest way when they are busy with the housework. A child reared in this way will develop a very fear-ridden moral sense, a very rigid super-ego, which does not develop into the mature sort of inner light that I was talking about.

You can see, that in marriage this sort of thing can cause immense problems. What part does this type of rigid moral sense play when husbands and wives come to war with each other? Because, as I have pointed out before, when you marry, in the end you have got to uncover. You can keep up a long courtship and never uncover, you can hide your essential self. But sooner or later, when you come to live with each other, you uncover your primitive self. Everything that is in you that is ultimately personal and rigid and personally demanding and arrogant and self-centered comes out in marriage. In marriage, people encounter the self. Sometimes many battles are fought between husband and wife and they are under the impression that they are battles between the two personalities, but it is frequently no such thing. It is a battle between the super-ego of the personalities rather than the personalities.

And sometimes marriages smash on this, and people separate from one another because the conflict has been with each other's poorly developed or rigid moral sense. Two aspects come out of a poorly developed moral sense. On the one hand the person can behave like a tyrant and on the other hand like a frightened child. The other person has to bear with a moral sense that is either harsh and demanding or a person who behaves like a subservient child. When a husband or wife see the qualities coming out they recoil in front of the revelation and begin to judge each other endlessly and secretly. This makes the love which should flow out to the mate flow back into the self. Whenever you withdraw love like that, it forms in you a tension and anxiety and creates states in which there is the expectancy of disaster ever at hand.

I read of an instance like that in a paper from Birkenhead, where I was long ago: A young mother of twenty-two committed suicide. She left a note to say that she owed rent for seventy-four pounds, and she got another summons for goods that very day, and she couldn't stick it any longer. She said in the note, 'If I could have gone to anybody, I'm sure it would have helped me, but I was afraid, dear, to come to you because I've been nasty to you this way for many years.' And in the evidence it was shown that many years ago she had overspent and her husband had forgiven her, and had been apparently kind. But she killed her three children as well. She gassed them. And you can see here the type of wrongly-developed moral sense we are talking about now. It showed that in spite of having babies, and that meant a sex relationship, the sex relationship wasn't at all harmonic or a profound relationship; and her attitude to her husband was one of fear and not of understanding. For whom should she have come to in that difficulty except her husband? The coroner praised the husband and said he obviously had been a very patient man and a nice man; but I think myself he had been an exceedingly blind man, and he paid a very heavy price for his blindness.

This is an instance of the kind of marriage I am talking about where this girl went a step further. She not only became passive in front of him, and fearful of him, but she took revenge in an unconscious way by running into debt. She did this unconsciously to injure him. And he was unaware of his lack of relationship with her, although he was married to her and they had three children. Now any number of men and women are in the position that the man has never known the joy of awakening his woman because his sadism and his identification with tyranny and tyrants has so overawed his little woman that she is afraid to show herself to him and in the end she can actually seek to be punished and criticised and be made to feel inferior. And yet such men make excellent men on committees, they make brilliant men in business, they have a great authoritative manner. But it is not true leadership, it is the command of fear. Therefore, if we men are going to awaken women so that we can truly say that we have fulfilled their lives, we must be careful not to repeat in our marriage the pattern of our own development. It could happen that we are not acting according to our true nature but according to our authoritarian father or teacher of old. And this element in us tries to overwhelm the essential self of the other person, they destroy their whole spirit, and they destroy the marriage. If you try to compel your wife or your husband not to be like themselves but to be like you or someone you like, you are offending against human relations and human personality, and you are preparing for immense conflict, insoluble conflict, in the marriage relationship. So it is important in the marriage relationship to make sure that we are conscious of acting in a mature way and not in any childish or tyrannical way, not behaving towards our wives or husbands the way our parents or teachers may have treated us when we were young.

ALOOF
AND
DEPENDENT

CHAPTER NINE

A very careful analysis carried out through many years of people who are psychologically disturbed shows that in a general way you can make a division of humanity into two basic types of individual, the aloof or dominant type and the dependent or submissive type of individual.

Let me show what I mean. As I said earlier when a person comes to be analysed at first they tend to develop a very warm relationship with the analyst who comes to be treated as if he were the parent or uncle or aunt who was the main influence on the patient during childhood. Now from this point onwards, the dependent type of individual leans increasingly on the analyst and shows more and more what you might call a childlike dependence on him. If there is any threat of breaking off the analysis, such people become very distressed, or if there is any feeling that the analyst is going to fail them, there is almost panic. And they live often enough in a state of unrest of spirit, because they are utterly dependent. Now when they are like that to the analyst, they're only giving in an exaggerated way their attitudes to everybody in their daily life. These people think very little of themselves. Everybody else is more important, everybody else is significant. They feel inferior. They feel unworthy. They feel no good. They feel helpless. And they suffer very much from this.

As a result, they do all they can to placate the people in their environment. They cannot bear to get into a state of anger with anybody in case the anger leads to a break and a separation. And therefore they stand a lot of bullying and a lot of hostility from people, and they are afraid. And they are afraid that if they show hostility things will go entirely wrong.

Now the aloof or dominant type is exactly the opposite. They are superior, detached, cold, not interested in people except in a superior way, looking down on everything. Their personality is the antithesis of the depending type. Such people are detached, isolated, and usually superior people. They consider most people inferior to themselves. They have quite a strong opinion of themselves, and they sustain through all their life this attitude of aloofness. Now people like that, wherever they live, form a problem for anyone who has got to live with them. For if you've got to live with a person who is cold, aloof, and unappreciative, you can suffer very much. Conversely, of course, you can also suffer with a person who is childish in their infinite dependence.

What happens when two such people marry? Imagine a marriage with this hidden attitude, where their two attitudes have been carefully hidden. We all try to hide these things that we sense are not nice in us. And two people come together and fall in love with each other, and then, when they come into the intimacy of human marriage, they can no longer cover up and they gradually reveal to each other this temperament and their nature. Now if, for example, a girl has got this dependence, after a few months of marriage, her husband is faced with the immense difficulty of having almost a child instead of a woman for his wife. She lives in a perpetual state of inferiority. She lives in a perpetual state of worry that she's not cooking the food properly, that she's not doing the household work properly, that she's not handling the finance of the house well enough, and she's bitterly critical of herself and looks up to her husband as a superior person. Now if he happens to be actually the opposite type to her and a very superior person, in a very short time a bitter dilemma arises between them. For the woman is clinging to a man who is aloof and indifferent and cold. If the woman is sexually quickened and awakened and would rejoice naturally and ecstatically in vivid sex relations, she's denied them by this man who, even if he has sex relations, can only offer her an indifference and a coldness and a superiority.

Now it's made equally problematic if the reverse is the case and the warm-hearted but dependent man marries a cold-hearted and non-dependent woman. The sex relationship then can be a tragic thing. For this man leans helplessly on his wife as if she were a mother. He can't bear to go out of her sight, can't bear to go out for a day, to a party or gathering of friends, wants to know where she is, her telephone number; can he ring up? can he find what she'd like? This is bad enough if the wife is sympathetic. But fancy a man being utterly dependent on a woman who can only answer him with independence and aloofness and coldness.

As a result of these attitudes, sooner or later quarrelling must spring up between these two types of people and they battle each other, for a girl or a boy who is utterly dependent can't understand this coldness, this aloofness, this superiority of the other person. And the superior person doesn't think they are aloof; they don't see their behaviour as anything other than normal and proper. They find the attentions of their mate annoying, particularly the sexual attentions; they want less and less sexual intimacy because they can't stand the closeness, the helplessness of it.

This situation is also very sad because it affects the children very much. Children are very sensitive to this sort of atmosphere in the home. And anyway, as the situation progresses, the aloof one may take to isolation more and more, locking themselves in rooms alone for hours. And their mate may go into a state of immense depression and anguish. Doctors are called in and give tranquillisers, which of course don't help the situation at all. All these do is prevent the coming to consciousness of the realities of the situation; and until these realities are got out into the open, drugs and tranquillisers only hide the symptoms and just further confuse the situation. Marriage counsel-

lors, doctors, priests, clergy, and interested people like that
who try to deal with such a situation have got to follow the
technique of the analyst in trying to solve the problem and
not merely endeavouring to reunite the man and woman
and stop them fighting each other. They must see that the
fight which is taking place in marriage is really a sham
fight. The real protagonists of the battle are the couple's
parents, not the husband and wife. I have seen a wife declare with all the power of her soul that she did not want
to see her husband again. I've seen her separated from her
husband, I've seen her thank God for the separation, and
she was absolutely sincere and meant it. There wasn't any
single sign of one kind of a thought that was otherwise.
I've seen that same girl three months afterwards in a state
of most profound anxiety about her husband, of an immense self-criticism of herself, of her ruthless analysis of
her own attitudes, and an aching and a longing to restore
relationship with her man. But if you'd listened to her and
believed everything she said, you would say that the relationship was utterly hopeless, from her point of view anyway, as she had expressed joy and relief in no longer being
in that relationship. You see, she was one of the dependent
type, who had leaned and leaned and leaned on her husband, and he was one of the aloof types, superior, and he
really was superior; so that when they first parted, there
was a sense of relief. She was no longer living with a perpetual critic. She was no longer leaning on or living with a
bully who watched everything and criticised everything.
But three months afterwards she was asking: 'Had she
caused this? Was she the cause of her man becoming like
this? She wished to God she could live with him again,
could see him, could talk the thing out with him. Could
she be frank for once in her life and say everything she
wanted to say?'

Now when a person such as this comes to the analyst,
the fact of being able to talk to a man or woman who tries
to understand, who tries to have an open heart and an
open mind, makes them feel so relieved at not being treated
in an inferior manner, at not being patronised, that they
respond at first exceedingly well. You might think the

problem was solved, that this augurs well for a rapid recovery; and analysts without experience may prophesy that they will perform a cure in six months, or nine months. But they don't know what they've touched. Such a person talks easily to anyone who will listen. But this initial outpouring must be exhausted before the real work of therapy can begin.

On the other hand, the opposite happens when the dominant type comes to analysis. He adopts an aloof, superior, contemptuous attitude to the analyst and the uninformed analyst might take this as an expression of sheer hostility. He could form the impression that it's going to be very difficult to heal this person because they appreciate nothing but themselves and value nothing except themselves. So the analysis becomes a painful experience for the analyst himself because he finds he has to stand by while every form of insult and contempt is richly heaped upon him. But if he has sufficient insight into his job, he knows that such people are ultimately not like that. They are the products of homes where parents have adopted similar attitudes towards their children and underneath the aloof exterior is a human being starved for the warmth of normal human relations.

I hope I've done enough to outline to you the type of character difference where you've either got a type of personality who leans on everybody and is weak themselves, broken-hearted if their mate goes away for a day or two, or on the other hand, the aloof type who would let their mate go away for a month and not miss him or her. In the face of separation, one feels lost without support, while the other feels jolly glad to get rid of this annoying, this clinging person. Quite often such people have to wait till death comes before they find their mistake. When a person who has been aloof and cold loses a mate whom they thought they didn't care about, the truth is suddenly brought home to them. Some people wait until death before enlightenment comes and I've had to bring people together sometimes and tell them that frankly if they did not find the way through now, they were going to be faced with some bitter circumstances in the future.

HANAGHAN'S
LAW

CHAPTER TEN

Now I want to talk about the tragic things that can happen when a child is reared in a home where the mother is away a lot and the child is reared by different people. I am thinking now particularly of our modern sophisticated homes where the mother is frequently absent and the children are left to nurses or servants.

Let me take an instance of what I have had in a number of cases in my analysis. Sophisticated fathers and mothers go on long continental holidays. They pack, go away, and leave their children to be taken care of by maids or nurses. Now I want you to see the confusion that is immediately introduced into the mind of a child. You will not understand it, however, unless you can imagine, those of you who are married, your own husband or wife packing up and sweetly kissing you and saying goodbye and leaving you for a month while they travelled themselves. But parents are amazingly blind and don't understand children this way. They don't realise all the love-yearning a child has for his parents. So a day comes when these God-like people which the child worships disappear and the child is shattered. Outwardly, of course, the child still looks the same, but if you could understand the spirit of the child, you would see that he is full of anguish and tension. At

first he cannot believe he is deserted, he cannot believe
he is left. He just suffers the utter agony of being cut off.
The object of his love-energy just vanishes. The child is
left with his love, but without his love object. What happens? Well, in the average sophisticated home, the child
at first may not even want to eat, because the mother who
was associated with feeding is gone. And when it over-
comes this link between mother and feeding, it may eat
but the love which would flow out to the mother is now
drawn back and pent-up in the child. Imagine a tank half-
full of water and then you fill it with extra water. Something like this happens: the child becomes overfull of himself and his love and becomes less aware of the environment.

What often happens at this stage is that the cook or the
househelp senses the problem and feels for the child. And
she will tease him with a little bit of food, she will offer
him this and she will offer him that and gradually try to
woo him. Without knowing it she is playing the role of a
psycho-analyst trying to heal the mind of the child. But
in doing this, she unwittingly draws the child unto herself. Now the child has two mothers, the mother who deserted him and who is educated and beautiful and the
woman who comforts him who is often uneducated and
maybe not so chic.

Here we have the splitting of the mother love of the
child. Instead of having one love to concentrate and live
for, the child now has two loves: the love of the mother
who has departed, which is also turning into hate, and the
love of the mother who has cared for him and has nursed
him and kissed him and has fondled him against her skirt
and against her bosom. The little fellow is drawn out and
he lives for a period in this new relationship of backstairs
and kitchen and so on. He does not want to be bothered
going to the other places in the house associated with the
sophisticated life of his parents such as the drawing-room,
which are so lonely.

Then his parents come back from holidays and the mother blithely thinks the child will rush out to meet her and
reach out his little arms to her. She is very annoyed when

the little chap sometimes does not even want to come and
look at her. He is not interested in her but is interested
deep down, but too hurt to say a word. So the mother is
up against a lover's problem; for just as a wife can be
terribly hurt if a new woman comes into her husband's
life, this mother is hurt because a new love has come into
her son's life. But she has got a very powerful weapon,
the weapon of authority. She becomes more condescending
towards the substitute mother and so the boy gradually
learns that the people who really love him are ordinary
people with whom the rest of his family will have no real
connection. By birth he belongs to the sophisticated, the
educated set, but his emotional support comes from the
housemaid. His love has gone out and attached itself to
the maid who cared for him when his mother deserted
him but his jealous mother, whom he also loves, adopts
such a condescending attitude to this person who is his sole
constant source of emotional support that he becomes confused and unhappy. Here is the dilemma: he cannot give
himself wholeheartedly to the loved one who rescued him;
he can only partially go to her because gradually he learns
that that part of the house should be visited as little as
possible. And so he grows up without any visible disturbance but all the while his emotional confusion is unresolved.
For he hates the mother whom he first loved but now has
learned to distrust, because in truth she is not fit to be en-
trusted with love. And yet he is compelled to look up to
her because she is authoritative and sophisticated. She can
afford money for fine dresses and fine ways and has all
sorts of 'chic' friends visit her, while his real love has none
of this finery. He is stuck with his problem and grows up
with a split in his emotional life. And this split can have
the most profound effects later on in life.

When a boy falls in love with a girl, what he does at first
is transfer the love he used to have to that girl. As a man
gets to know his woman, he should develop a love for her
that becomes authentic in its own right. And coming to
love someone in this mature way is a long hard process. In
my judgement, it takes at least ten years to forge a beautiful union like that, where there is no longer pretence or

bluff or anything hidden. That is the normal thing. Now take the case of our chap from the sophisticated home. His choice of girl will depend on which of his mothers he loved most. Supposing it is the housemaid! He falls in love with a girl of similar type and feels as if heaven has come back to him because he gets a similar type of affection as that which he got from the old housemaid, warm and loving. So he marries the girl who will most likely be from a lower social class. Shape of body, attitudes of mind, interests and so on, lead him to such a marriage. And initially, he may have a very beautiful marriage. He has children and everything seems fine. The in-laws get to know one another and things seem to be working out okay. But all is not well because only one of his mother-loves has gone over to this girl. The ties with his sophisticated mother are still there, repressed. What can happen?

Sometimes, after such a man has been married for years, a woman walks into a room where he is and some toss of her head, some mannerism of hers, some aristocratic demeanour, something authentic of the ancient days cuts across his memory like lightening flashing in the dark. To his own amazement, an immense surge of feeling which he cannot understand arises within him. He is aware that he is rapturously falling in love and his own wife seems common in comparison with this lady; she becomes debunked in his eyes. Ancient glory falls from her and onto this other woman, beautiful, maybe cruel and ruthless—in fact, sometimes chosen because of her ruthlessness as well as her beauty, because his mother was ruthless as well as beautiful. The man may then start an affair with the woman and pour all the passion of his life into the relationship and the love that took him to his first wife disappears like a river going underground.

He is tremendously troubled and he strives and fights and vacillates. Sometimes he will come home to his wife and she has made a beautiful meal, beautifully done and ready for him, and it awakens the ancient, unconscious memory of how the maid fed him when he was wretched and his mother was away. He feels a sudden swell of affection; he has passionate and joyous sex relations with

her, and the other self is utterly eclipsed and forgotten. He
wonders how the hell he could have bothered with her and
when he meets her the next time he wonders and he is on
guard and tragically troubled; and the woman herself is
stirred. Then, if the tragedy goes on, these two women
set out each of them to get this man. They do not come
together, or practically never come together; they never
seek any understanding by which two women could come
together and talk this thing out. They are on guard against
each other, alert and hostile and bitter and sneering at
each other.

One or the other of them may become ruthless. His
working-class wife may suddenly flash and become what
his imagination tells him that she is, common and coarse.
He finds he has got a tyrant of a wife, not the placid,
simple love he first imagined her to be. So, now he faces
a gigantic struggle, a gigantic problem. I may say that
very few men or women are capable of resolving this problem for it will never be brought to a true issue until these
two women come together and understand one another.
Otherwise there is nothing but ruthless and secret war.
This is the problem when the love drive is split and it is a
common one amongst the upper classes in most countries.
No man or woman is healthy psychologically who is only
giving part of their love to their wife or to their husband.
I can be perfect as a lover to my wife and give her every
consideration and be tender with her and convince her of
my affection; but if there is a part of my love repressed
and pushed out, if I have another love, another mother of
olden days, the repressed love can come up at any time and
destroy our relationship.

It is precisely the same if the reverse takes place and a
boy marries a sophisticated, proud woman who has the
dignity and often the class relationship that makes her a
perfect image of his sophisticated mother. The boy can
pour out all his love on such a girl, can marry her in style
if you like, have the Brigade of Guards out to grace the
marriage, photographs taken, reports of the marriage put
into the paper. The man can be honestly and warmly in
love with his wife, and may for two or three years live

what you would call a completely happy and whole life.

But repressed in his unconscious mind is the memory of a more simple woman, of a more homely woman, of a more friendly woman, a woman more close to life who cares what he eats and takes care of him. And such a woman coming into his ken can suddenly create an upsurge of long-hidden emotion. And he can be shattered by it and fall deeply in love with this girl and smash his marriage. Some men get so desperate in this situation that, instead of being able to resolve their problem, they start associating with prostitutes. For to these men, the prostitute is the working-class woman whom their mother despised. Many such men go to prostitutes because they need the love of a working-class girl; only with these girls do they find comfort.

This pattern of distortion of love in the upper classes has caused great suffering throughout the whole history of aristocracy in Europe and America. It has shattered house after house and brought sorrow and pain. It has left coldness and aloofness and hostitlity instead of love. For in the end, when a man is swayed by this ambivalence of loves he becomes tired and weary and permanently perplexed. For the truth is that our marriage pattern does not fulfil man's nature. We have tried in our hypocrisy to compel men and women into the form of marriage that we have made and called divine, just like the hypocrites in Jesus' time called the Sabbath divine and compelled the people to fit in with this. But marriage was made for man and not man for marriage.

But what kind of creative organisation of society are men and women going to make in order that children will not walk into these disasters and smash their lives, generation after generation after generation? Love is the use of intelligence in its highest order; love is the fearless investigation of evidence with an open mind as to where the evidence will lead. And just as science would be a bastard science if it tried to manipulate the facts and fit them to its own ends, so is religion a bastard religion until it is brave enough and sensible enough and mighty enough to take account of the whole problem of human life.

Can you see how sad is the picture I have just given to you? Can't you see how pathetic it is that these people are all sincere? When the man fell in love with his working-class wife, he was utterly sincere. He did not know he was divided. And when he swings the other way, he still thinks he is sincere and not divided in any way. But deep down in the heart is the rift, the absolute division; and nothing can be done until we find a way to talk frankly to one another and tell each other what we feel.

Let men and women have the courage to talk to each other. Let them have the courage to tell each other what they think. Let a man have the courage to tell his wife and let his wife have the courage to tell her man what she thinks, because once you start to think, you start to alter; once you start to think genuinely, you start improving the whole of human society. But it can only be done through sincere, brave, honest thinking. And that is why I again turn to Jesus of Nazareth who said, 'Seek and ye shall find; knock and it shall be opened unto you.' Jesus was the first who taught the way of seeking and investigation: 'Seek and ye shall find; knock and it shall be opened unto you.'

TRIPTYCH

CHAPTER ELEVEN

The sexual nature of man has three facets, a biological, a sociological, and a spiritual. Therefore, man has three fundamental hungers, one to fulfill his biological need, one to fulfil his sociological purpose, and a third one uniquely related to the individual spirit of man, the necessity to enter into relationships with a trans-mural or trans-mortal universe, with an immortal spiritual kingdom. Only when all three needs are fulfilled is man truly man. Many relationships between men and women are utterly destructive because they take one of these facets of man's nature to be the whole thing. Many marriages and many courtships are wrecked because people attend solely to the biological hunger in their personalities, and they go into their relationships with impassioned beauty and the absolute certainty that they have achieved something utterly vital; and they have. They are sure that they have found some magically beautiful thing because they have found a mate with whom they can physically, sexually live. And, whilst the biological mood is upon them, they have great happiness and delight. No one can fail to see the glory and the beauty of such biological unity. And if man were no more than a biological animal, such fulfilment would be the satisfaction of life.

But man's sex has a sociological aspect. Within the heart of every man and woman is the desire to see one's own child. Even when we repress this, when illness or psychological disturbance makes us mock the idea, in the soul of every human being, there is a desire to see their own children inheriting the land. There is a desire to welcome and bring into relationship little children. Our whole political, educational and economic set-up springs from this fundamental wish in the human heart.

And many people have entered into marriage or sex relations with a very clear understanding of this aspect of their natures. They plan their families and arrange for the culture and education of their children, linking this living generation to the generations that have been, tying the living child to all the values which our civilisation has inherited from evolution and history. And some find in the fulfilment of this task a whole life's work.

But marriage or sex relations which go no further than this leave one of the deepest hungers of man unfulfilled, the hunger of the spirit. Man is not the product of his environment and his heredity; man inherits his heredity and his environment and his spirit combats both these mighty forces in an attempt to achieve a richer, profounder, and more excellent life. Deep down in the heart of man, whether he be Mohammedan, Catholic, Protestant, or Jew, is a hunger for the perfect beauty, for the perfect love, for the perfect truthfulness which is never found on earth. You can go to no institution, no place wherein you will find the fulfilment of that hunger. It is even in the heart of a woman as she sits with a child on her knee and surrounded by economic and cultural security. Deep in the heart of each man and woman is this ache for the utmost love. And many quarrels which occur in homes, many tragic differences which emerge in home life are due to this feeling of spiritual loneliness where the individual finds that he or she is not fully gratified. And we turn on our mates and blame them secretly for this nonfulfilment and our mate unaware is blaming us in the solitary and profound way.

The human heart is not gratified by orgastic fulfilment;

neither is it gratified by the sociological satisfaction of splendid cultural achievements such as the glorious civilisations of the past. Man is still hungry, still wistful, still inevitably lonely. He has a sense of not being understood even by the person who comes closest to him. Man and wife in the moments of their deepest embrace are as islands set apart in an ocean. There is no fulfilment unless such people learn that, just as the biological wish has its fulfilment and the sociological wish has its fulfilment, in a similar way the fulfilment of the spiritual life depends upon the discovery of the religious experience. A man can be quite blind and a woman can be quite blind to this requirement. It is possible to go, not only day by day but month by month and year by year, and push away from the centre of consciousness this deepest, profoundest, most mysterious longing of the human heart, and yet I declare to those of you who are married and have reached what you think is the highest fulfilment of a successful marriage, I know you lie to yourself if this inner life of perfection has not found some fulfilment and some expression and some factual incarnation.

Now, home is the only place where all three of these basic requirements in man can be fulfilled. Home is a necessity for man, not that men and women may dwell together for a short space of years, but that they may live out in its fullest excellence the fulfilment of their natures.

If I am right, my analysis should throw some light on many things which perplex us in our modern civilisation. The present modern generation has seen the overthrow of conventional home-life and conventional sexual relations. Beginning with the disturbances of the first World War and accompanied by the iconoclastic brilliance of George Bernard Shaw and Ibsen and other men of letters, the hypocrisy of the European home was thoroughly exposed, and young men and women began sexual experiments which have spread over the whole of Europe and America. The idea of a preliminary courtship in which the phsyical side of sex is restrained has practically disappeared from European thought and conduct, and there has been an immense increase of sexual experiment, often guided by blind

guides like Marie Stopes. And unfortunately, many people
have sat at the feet of such prophetesses, and instead of
wisdom have inherited a world of confusion.

But when the conventions were overthrown, man was
not free as he thought. All he did was substitute one tyranny for another, the external tyranny of convention for the
internal tyranny of distorted impulse. In truth and honesty we renounced the external rules which bound us and
laughed at them, and we had a right to laugh at them. We
then thought we were free and the joy of doing things we
were not allowed to do was so glorious and so satisfactory
that we couldn't possibly look at the danger that it involved. But in truth we gave up the external conventions
which were holding us only to become the serfs of our unknown, titanic, interior forces.

Society was now in the grip of a raw biological life-force
which was very much in evidence in the literature of the
period when this movement began. But those of us who
are psycho-analysts know that when the biological impulses
drive you to mating, they don't drive you from spirit to
spirit, from person to person; they drive you according
to the complexes or fixations of your childhood and you
gravitate towards the people whose complexes in some way
answer your own. It is not the free choice of love which
people like to imagine it is. It is unconscious and occurs
almost without understanding. Many marriages are made
on this basis; the courtships are short, vital, and joyous
and the rapture of the first marriage years is marvelous.
But because these people have to continue living with each
other they make a second discovery. When you can get all
there is to get out of physical sex, there is still no fulfilment. The sociological needs of the couple begin to be felt
and this may give rise to quarrels and discontent with each
other. In some cases, the bitter quarrels which unveil this
need lead to further understanding. But in others they
lead to evasion of the issue, or even living apart. Such
people may meet maybe once or twice a month and when
they meet it's glorious because they don't have to encounter the total will and spirit and personality of the other.
They gratify each other's bodies and they have a joy in the

gratification of the body, but they leave untouched, unexplored, and unsatisfied the far, far deeper human sexual need of home, of a child in the home, of the struggle of different outlooks in the education of the child, and of the differences that must be faced in order that the truth may emerge between the two people. The biological sex relationship never comes under the discipline of the sociological and tragically this leads very easily to promiscuity.

When men, for instance, who have become promiscuous in this way, return home exhausted, their wives present them with the actual sociological problem of two different people living together. And they become unable to bear the tension of such a fight but secretly day-dream about their other lover, imagining all sorts of beautiful and rapturous scenes. They live a life of phantasy, investing their lover with imaginative qualities which are the result of their own desires. In the end they can stick it no longer and many of them marry their biological lover, with disastrous results. American statistics show that seventy per cent of divorced people go back to make love again to their first partner, and with tragic results because that first magic can never be recaptured. They are trying to find a biological solution for what is essentially a sociological or spiritual problem.

Our generation is afflicted with this unfortunate tendency to seek a biological relationship only and they cannot endure the patience that is required even in biological mating, so they continue to gravitate to people who will give them a fulfilment that is delightful, but short-term and incomplete. But in this way they develop a rift between their phantasy life and their marriage. In their imaginations, they live a secret and unreal love life. They engage in the fulfilment of the most perfect love dreams and return to reality deflated, unable to withstand the labour of living with somebody. Their home is robbed of social and spiritual power, of hallowedness, and their children suffer starvation of the soul. So these biological lovers bring mildew and disaster to the essential spirituality of home life.

When people have the courage to face up to the sociological battle of living together, then they will build a home

not just of four walls containing a number of rooms, but
a place where excellence is achieved in the building of that
wider life where children get the cultural education that
guarantees full development.

If you face your mate honestly, you will discover at first
the immense differences between you. But there is more to
it than that. Both men and women have a basic drive of
self-will, so that again and again the deepest elements of
their natures clash, if they are sincere. Home is not a place
of rest; it is a place of peace. But peace is the fruit of
sincere conflict. And if you are prepared to work for this
peace, to come face to face with the irrational element in
man and woman, you will find your mate is weaving
dreams that would destroy a civilisation, never mind a
home. You look into the mirror of truth and you see hate
and darkness. But if you're honest, you'll discover something also, a feeling that it shouldn't be so. You'll become
aware that you can surmount this crisis. You sense that it
would be better for you to die serving this thing than live
denying it. You begin to know the meaning of the Cross,
the meaning of acceptance, of accepting a burden as the
essential of your humanity, that life is not a rationalistic
system but a sacrificial system. You come to realise that the
only person who can save your mate is you, the only person
who can stand sane in the hour of ultimate crisis is you.
And the realization becomes a prayer. Prayer is not uttered
by choice. Prayer is the soul's necessity. When you're spiritually bankrupt, when you have no answer on earth to this
particular problem, your cry is your prayer. You can't
argue; you can't be logical; you can't say, 'Let us talk it
out'; you can't say, 'Be fair'; you can't say, 'Let us be
rational.' You can only take the soul of your mate into
your keeping and without revenge, argument, or justifica-
tion, you just abide. And because you abide, your mate is
assured that whatever madness or failure grips her soul,
she will be assured of one who abides in understanding and
pity. And you will begin to realise the ultimate function
of marriage, your mutual redemption. And how beautiful
it is when overwhelmed by conflict, you see tenderness in
the eyes of the woman from whom you expected nothing

but anger and argument. At such moments you will understand the mystery of the Incarnation, the Kingdom of Heaven come on earth; for only then are you really married, only then are you assured of something everlasting and eternal in the midst of time. You will discover that the orgastic pleasure of sex is only a very dim symbol of the spiritual ecstasy which comes to a man and a woman when they have been through these difficulties and see each other for the first time eye to eye and spirit to spirit.

If I could persuade a group of people to look inside and find out if what I have said is true; if I could persuade a group of people to experiment and test this life, then I would have no doubt that from such a group would spring the profoundest religious regeneration that has been known on this earth for probably two thousand years. The tragedy is that our civilisation has lost the idea of the hallowed; our children grow up spiritually lonely; and our adults remain immature because they harken only to one of the three aspects of the nature of man.

SEQUESTERED STREAMS

CHAPTER TWELVE

Freud was the first one to classify a group of illnesses which he called the 'anxiety neuroses.' And he did this back in the 1880's. Let me tell you some of the symptoms of this condition so that you will see that it is much more widespread than you might think.

The most common aspect is a general state of anxiety, needless anxiety. For example, a woman might have a fear that her husband would be knocked down by a car on the way home for lunch; or a man at work might be all the time worried that his wife was seriously ill. With the slightest upset in life, such a person gets immensely excited or troubled. They also suffer from irritability, sleeplessness, possibly an excessive fear of specific things such as heights and even, in bad cases, from a persistent fear of insanity. As well as these psychological symptoms they may have intestinal trouble, bowel disturbances, stomach pains, rheumatic trouble, arhythmic beating of the heart, or even angina. They may also suffer from excessive hunger so that they eat and eat but are never satisfied. Unaccountable perspiration is also another common symptom. Now all these signs seem to be very different, but in most cases an analyst can prove that they stem from something basic gone wrong with the

spiritual or psycho-sexual life of the person. What sort of
basic problem could this be? Let me give you an example
from my own experience. A man came to me who was
in quite an anxious state. The case was very puzzling at
first until one thing gave me a clue. He had only one
child and that child was nineteen years old. By probing a
bit further, I found that the real cause of his illness was
the practice of 'coitus interruptus,' that is, instead of having a normal, adequate sexual relationship, the man withdraws leaving his woman ungratified. Now the trouble
with his behaviour is that it takes five, six, and maybe
ten years before its effects become obvious. For example, Freud noticed that most divorces occurred around the
ninth and tenth years of marriage and he ascribed this to
some hitch in the psycho-sexual life of the couple. Because it takes so long to have obvious effects, the first in-
timation of the root cause of the anxiety that the analyst
may have is the startling declaration by the patient that
he has no sexual desire. At first it is a little hard to believe that the couple have not had sexual relations for
months and were not interested in having any. But it
gradually becomes certain that this is in fact the situation.

Now what is the connection between a perverted sex
life and the anxiety condition I am talking about? Freud
noted that in normal sexual relationships, certain things
occur such as an increased heart-beat, much perspiration,
extensive use of the tactile senses and a general excitement of the body. Now the sexual act runs a normal
course through to fulfilment and the end result is that
the partners fall lovingly and peacefully to sleep together.
Now imagine what will happen when you interrupt twenty, thirty, forty, maybe hundreds of such love-making
sessions. All the excitement mobilised for the act is time
and again prevented from running its normal course
through to release and a state of equilibrium. The energy gradually becomes displaced from the sex act to all
sorts of other situations, giving rise to unaccountable
heart disturbance, skin afflictions, and a whole host of
psychosomatic conditions. And the sexual act itself becomes dreary and uninteresting. Just as when you block

a river and it goes that way, and you block it again and it goes another way, similarly, when you block the sexual life through an artificial relationship, nature tries to put it right and these other conditions are really an attempt at energy release.

I had one case of a woman who had been treated repeatedly for Graves disease which kept coming back. I suspected she was having some form of incomplete love with a man. She was the headmistress of a school and unmarried, and when I suggested to her that she was having a relationship with a man she shouted, 'You dirty, filthy thing!' picked up her umbrella and stormed out of the house, slamming the door. I knew I was right. But I was a bit troubled and I asked the parson with whom I was staying about it, and he said he'd make enquiries— she was one of his congregation. She spoke to him and he said that she told him I had interested her but my fee would be far too high. Well, I knew she had no money at the time because she was keeping her mother in a nursing home, so I sent my compliments back to her and said my fee would be a penny, and that I thought it would be worth her while seeing me. A few days later she came and instead of being arrogant and holding her head in the air, she said, 'How did you know I had a man?' That was her greeting to me: 'How did you know I had a man?' Well, as a result, I got to know all about her situation and I was able to heal her.

Apart from these sorts of distressing situations, very often young lovers married only three or four years become bored stiff with each other sexually. And if the woman is left sexually hungry and the man is left without any sexual capacity, she may begin to have contempt for her husband for she thinks he is impotent. He isn't, of course, it's just that his energies have become displaced into other pursuits. One of the tragic things about such men and women is that they have very little frank conversations about their sex life. To bring their problems and dissatisfactions out into the open is the beginning of the solution.

Now unfortunately, our civilisation so over-emphasises

the physical side in sexual relationship that the real essence in male-female relationships is lost. Love is essentially a spiritual relationship between two people.

Freud thought this was so mysterious that in order to explain it he had the picture of two people, say the woman living in England and the man living in Ireland, by some mysterious telepathic process through many years gradually approaching till they physically met and that these two lovers made one, where each before had only been half. A very beautiful picture! These people were drawn by the spirit, by the love, not by the physicality at all, although the physicality is there: they were drawn to each other by some mysterious force which even Freud himself failed to understand. And many men who are well mated, and many women who are well mated, feel that this is indeed a mystery because when they turn back and ask, 'How did I ever meet you, and how did you ever meet me?' it looks as if they never could have met except by a series of unaccountable accidents. But once they are drawn together the first relationship is the communion of their hearts.

Now this is the sex relationship I'm talking about, the true sex relationship and any other is partial and inadequate. The first encounter is a relationship of beauty and love, of shy beauty and shy love where the woman feels that she wants to surrender her whole being to this particular man and this particular man feels that this woman is queenly and wonderful and beautiful; it is as if he has new eyes and he penetrates into the mysterious depths of womanhood for the first time; and she, like the sleeping beauty in the story, awakens to her own beauty. As Spenser pointed out in his very beautiful love poems, a lover in telling his beloved how beautiful she is actually awakens her sleeping beauty to real, creative life and she becomes what he mirrors: he holds with his love the mirror of love to her and she beholds her countenance and she knows she is that lovely being, but she did not know it until he told her.

Can't you see the difference, the immense difference, between our modern conception of sensual love and the

thing I am talking about? Can't you see the immense
difference? This is some intimacy of inner heart, somebody that comes along for the first time can open the
doors of the treasure-house of your woman's spirit; magically for the first time a man has come, spoken to you,
and before you know where you are, you are disrobing
your spirit; and the disrobing of the spirit should always
precede the disrobing of the body; to disrobe the body
for any other reason but in answer to the disrobing of the
spirit is prostitution, whether it is inside marriage or not.
For this is the essence of the love relationship of the spiritual side and it is when you feel this mysterious lover
seeing right into the woman depths of your being, and
you have the new insight to see into the depth of his being and his soul, that you both want to touch each other.
If it is only to touch with your finger tip the curl of the
hair of the woman, if you only want to touch with a finger tip the shoulder, this is the touch, this is the preliminary to the sensual side of love. A sensualist can never
awaken the whole woman and neither can a sensual woman awaken the whole man.

Now when you have a relationship based on these principles, the idea of 'coitus interruptus' is fatal! The idea
of withdrawing, the idea of being parsimonious and fearful is completely alien to real love-making.

And the result of incomplete love-making affects more
than a man's relations with his woman. It affects his relations with everyone including his men friends, because
he withdraws into himself and becomes narcissistic and
anxious. He becomes hostile to everyone including those
at his place of work, with the result that many such men
give up lucrative jobs and continually change their em-
ployment. Many of these people become invalids and develop cancer, severe headaches, stomach trouble, and have
all sorts of dreads and fears. They also become arrogant
and rude even to their own children.

The best advice an analyst can give such people is to
become celibate for several months and embark upon a
programme of good diet and exercise to restore their systems to normal. In doing this they must wait for the

dawn again of spiritual love when the partners will move towards each other, not to forceful, intimate sex, but to come again to the point where they want to touch a curl of hair or a shoulder or a hand in beauty and love.

Now, if you will do that, I can assure you you will have great joy, for then you will be able to live, not only in the sacrament of love, but you will have a sensuality that the sensualist has not got the slightest dream of; you will be able to have a physical delight and fulfilment that the ordinary sensual man can never experience. 'Seek first the Kingdom of Heaven and its glory and all these other things shall be added unto you.' Seek the love, seek the yearning for each other on the basis of spiritual love, and all these other things shall be given to you.

CHASTITY

CHAPTER THIRTEEN

The modern emphasis on physical beauty with its myriads of beauty preparations makes its difficult for me to comprehend that there wasn't always this accent on the physical or bodily aspect of things. We know so much about the flesh now that we get blasé about it; we know so much about the body that we get bored with it. But if you read the early poetry of Ireland, England, and the continent, you will find that men were aware of woman, not just as a physical entity, but as a mysterious thing, intangible and spiritual. They were allured by spiritual attractiveness, by loveliness unstated; they were enamoured of the intangible and not the tangible; they were in love with the invisible man or woman and not the physically visible. In some ways they had an almost childlike unawareness of the body; they made no investigations and would not have understood them if they had. They were immensely shy in front of each other. But nowadays we are scallywags and teddyboys in our impertinent knowledge and there goes with this the irreverence that is the mood of the hour. There are very few men and women who have a sense of continued reverence in each other's presence and yet that should be the fundamental relationship. For a woman's body is not the woman, as you well know if you love her and she dies; her form is still there, the flesh is still there, but you know that something has evaporated, something has gone, and it is not just the stopping of the heart and of the life-function. Here is someone who came to you with sparkling eye, somebody who sometimes came to you with angry eye, someone living and vivid, spiritual being in touch with spiritual being. You felt the encounter with personality, with the sacredness of personality even if at times it were a personality of anger and passion.

But our sensual era no longer thinks this way. We worry instead about the mechanics of sex, how best to achieve sexual expression. Have you ever seen an article in any of the women's magazines or men's magazines on the sanctity of chastity, on chastity as being one of the fundamental elements of love, an instrument of love, a message of love? What would be the reaction of most people nowadays even at the mention of the word 'chastity'? Would they sneer, smile, or maybe just squirm? Mention chastity, and most people think of nuns! Because of this I want to discuss this topic of chastity. And when I speak of chastity, I mean it in the broadest sense.

Long before the Roman Empire collapsed in the military sense, her spiritual life had decayed. This decay showed itself in the excessive cruelty that became rife and the general corruption of sexual life which was everywhere to be seen. These were manifestations of a gradual dying out of the sense of the sacred or holy; chastity was passé! The void which was left gave rise to the adoption of many religious and philosophic movements, of which Christianity eventually became the most influential. And it became the most influential because those who professed it were prepared to die rather than do otherwise. And the early Christian attitude towards sex was one of renunciation and repression which gave rise to the vast medieval network of convents and monasteries. So the swing from a complete absence of chastity at the end of the Roman Empire was towards a massive adoption of a repressive form of chastity in the middle ages. At the same time the tradition of medieval chivalry developed, which was originally an attempt by men to govern their impulses towards women and to treat relations between the sexes with reverence.

In art, the chief manifestation of this movement was the appearance of the Virgin Mary in the role of both virgin and mother. Whereas in the Roman civilisation, the accent was on the voluptuous ecstasy of the physical delights of Venus, in the Christian era the approach to women was expressed in works of art which featured the Virgin Mary for the most part. And the accent on the Virgin Mary arose not from the idea of celibacy as we know it today. It was an endeavor to get a pure conception of womanhood.

But I think this whole attempt at chastity through repression failed and gave rise to an outpouring of masochism and sadism in art and history. One of the first signs of failure was the appearance of sentimental paintings such as those of Christ crucified with thorns in His head and blood flowing down His face. These paintings began to show the lack of understanding of the reality of things which goes along with the repression of any part of man's real nature. And of course the sadism was all too evident in the savagery of the Inquisition, which in turn gave rise to massive reactions to authoritarian systems such as the French Revolution. So it seems to me that the whole problem of chastity and sexuality has been handled very badly by European man so far.

Now, if we really want to get a hint of the meaning of chastity, it would help us first not to think in terms of sexuality at all, but in terms of the meaning of chaste as used in art. For instance, the furniture in this room is not chaste, it is ornate; it is Austrian carved wood made by the same man who made the furniture for the Emperor Joseph of Austria. It is very far from chaste and it shows the mental conflict inherent in humanity. Here is the Royal head, the stern, authentic ruler, who dominates the whole scene. And here is the base for the Royal Arms of authority and down here he appears symbolically as a lion's head and you will find that the teeth are carved. Great furniture! but in no way chaste or refined.

It exudes the idea of government by authority, of government by some overwhelming agency. Massive Norman architecture similarly conveys the sense of the massive authority of God; the great solid walls, the huge pillars, the colossal weight contrast with the littleness of man.

When Gothic architecture sprang up originally around Austria, only a few men at first were master-builders of the Gothic and they had the idea not just of solid weight, of great mass and majesty which was akin, of course, to Egyptian architecture, but of grace and beauty, of balance and function; in other words, they had the idea of chastity. The great Gothic masters sought to get a dynamic conception of building by poise and balance, one set of powers here caught by the opposite and the keystone in between balancing two dynamic opposites. They did not have the idea of holding things by weight but by counter-balance, the buttress and the flying buttress harmonically balanced one against the other, rearing something higher and higher with the idea of capturing the beauty of the heavens, the beauty of God dwelling in the building; and they made use, as you know, of shafts of light through windows of various shapes so that the gloom of their roofs would be illumined by the sunshine, and when they used stained-glass windows the beauty became more and more manifest.

At first, these Gothic buildings were full of grace and beauty but, as Ruskin pointed out, the pride of the different builders led to pollution of the original ideas. The vanities that came into Gothic art sprang from man's interior vanity and the chaste, refined, balanced thing passed away.

Now the interesting thing is this: if you succeed in making a chaste building or a chaste poem, something happens. It is not only that you have made something that is beautiful; it is that these buildings, these poems actually act as cups, if you like, for holding the diviner wine. Something happens to these chaste works of art which never happens to the ornate. When men stand in front of a chaste work of art, they become aware almost of a spiritual silence surrounding them, they do not want to speak much; they want to gaze on this picture, or on that building, or on the beautiful carved figure; and as they stand before it, this inanimate thing seems to whisper something sacred to man. And it is the chastity and refinement of the work which achieves this effect.

Now, if this is true about works of art, the highest work of art that is produced is man himself, for the art of living is the most difficult of all the arts and wherever you meet a man or a woman who contains within himself or herself this sense of the holy, this sense of the pure, this sense of the lovely, you then have met a person who has learned chastity and its meaning.

And this is very much what we in modern times have to learn. Until we learn the meaning of chastity in our sexual life, we will have no access to a sense of the holy, no access to a sense of loveliness and purity.

The clearest manifestation today of our attitudes towards sex is the way we talk about it. I wonder do people realise the harm done by clever dirty jokes, for example. How many men realise that when they tell dirty stories in the club, they cannot come home and have pure sexual relations with their women? One of the saddest things today is the lack of reverence for the sexual relationship, this lack of chastity. I believe that the fundamental beginning of all disturbance in the sexual life is in the tongue, because with this idle and loose conversation, we are polluting the imagination. Loose sexual talk and sensuality are likewise not an abuse of the flesh but of the imagination. Now when men and women face each other, they can do so with reverence as they did in the Garden of Eden, or with a curse on their hearts where they cast themselves out of Eden, and turned away from their own loveliness. I do not think that any man or woman can remain satisfied with any sexual expression that is not a sacrament of beauty and love. A true sexual life is chaste; it is the expression of a reverence and an attraction and a yearning of one's spiritual mate.

If people learn that the true sexual relationship is a contact between the spiritual nature of man and woman, then the sense of touch which is the most intimate of languages, instead of just awakening a physical body, declares a sensitive and delicate worship for the woman who is being caressed. When the touch is not to awaken the passion of another, but to seek her spirit of which the body is just the veil, then it becomes music which is sacred, satisfying, and infinite. When touch is the spirit's eloquence, the sexual embrace becomes the final sacramental escape from the self-love. And in that experience, we know the meaning of chastity, because we see that, like the furniture mentioned earlier, any flourescent play, any inadequate bombast, which may be very attractive and very powerful, does not communicate anything except coldness in the end.

THE THREE
FACES OF
ADAM

CHAPTER FOURTEEN

Modern man tends to thinks of things in general and the sex relationship in particular very much on the biological level. But I want to show that all this biological information about sex is not bringing us one whit closer to an understanding of real man-woman relationships. For when you know all about Fallopian tubes and the menstrual cycle and all about spermatozoa, you know nothing at all about man as man and woman as woman and still less about man and woman as mates for each other, for though the relationship between men and women is mediated through their bodily forms, they are ultimately a mystery to each other. It was never intended that man should solve woman; she is the wild unsolvable thing. It was never intended that woman should solve man; he is the unsolvable force in her life. Counterpoised against each other they present a mystery, the resolution of which is to be achieved not by attempting to transcend it with knowledge but by abiding with each other through everything. The need of this generation is to remove this great emphasis on sexual knowledge which we have developed and which is destroying us because it is giving us a completely narrow biological view of man and woman. For all we know about sex I don't know of any age that was so bankrupt of real sexual understanding. To discuss some of the reasons for this I want to go back to an old and very beautiful story, the story of the 'Sleeping Beauty.'

The theme of the story is that of a young and beautiful girl who must remain asleep until the right man, the prince, comes along and wakens her with a kiss. Of course such a story is quite obviously not referring to her being physically asleep; what it means is that the girl is sexually asleep and cannot be awakened until some particular prince comes along and awakens her. What happens when the prince comes along and kisses her? Now the answer isn't that she then gets agitated and wants to go to bed with him; it isn't that she gets agitated and wants physical sex which she can hardly control. That would be the answer of modern so-called freethinkers. For what the girl feels is a sense of immense wonder and immense beauty, a sense of awakening as out of sleep, with horizons of an ineffable future opening out in front of her which she never knew about before. For this 'prince' has filled her world full of promise; for the first time she is really aware of herself and her potential as a woman. It is the right of every girl in truth to experience such an awakening. But it is also my belief that a large number never undergo the experience of being awakened. The sad truth is that thousands of couples live together, have sexual relations and even children, while all the while the woman has never been awakened, her real personality, her real sexual life lies dormant, untapped. What would happen if our modern mind could rediscover the real meaning of the story of the 'Sleeping Beauty'? How would it come about? Well, we know the sleeping beauties are there, so the problem seems to be the matter of the proper kind of princes to awaken them! What is it about men that does or doesn't awaken the real nature of women? Where do they go wrong, so that so many 'sleeping beauties' remain dormant?

I remember once listening to a particular orchestra playing, and hearing the same orchestra a week later but this time conducted by Sir Thomas Beecham. The difference was phenomenal; it was hard to believe it was the same orchestra. The point I want to make is this: two things are involved in such an orchestral performance; one is the potential within the orchestra itself and the other is the insight of the conductor into the work. A really great conductor has a profound insight into the music, not just a knowledge of the mechanics of orchestral music. Some conductors are efficient in the technique of music, efficient in the mathematical potentialities of the music. In other words, they are tonally brilliant, brilliant in their insight into the pure mechanical form of music, its cadences, its contrasts, its discords, and so on. But there are other men who have an intuition that the music itself is really symbolic, that it is a whisper in the dark, that it is telling us something. The great conductor then draws out the real meaning of the particular music by sensing and knowing the potentialities of the men and women in the orchestra. And we are happy when we find a man who has both the musical skill and spiritual intuition to achieve this.

Now when a man falls in love with a woman, the kind of results he gets depends on what kind of a conductor he is. Woman is such a complicated creature that it requires the skill and understanding of a really good conductor to bring her into the understanding and harmony and synthesis of a genuine sex relationship, to awaken the 'Sleeping Beauty.' Is her partner man enough to appeal to the very centre of her being or can he only engage certain aspects of her personality? The answer to this question depends on how mature the man is; it depends on the manner in which he has succeeded in combining the three main aspects which Freud called the 'id,' his conscious self or 'ego,' and his conscience or 'super-ego.' The mature person will have integrated these three aspects of himself so that neither one of them is particularly dominant. But unfortunately not everyone achieves this synthesis. According to how men have been conditioned by early training at home and subsequent development one or other of these three aspects of the person may be dominant and their approach to women will be governed by this factor.

But supposing a boy has been brought up by very strict people who have made him arrogant? He identifies himself with some of the tyrants of his own upbringing. He comes to a woman with a dominant super-ego or conscience and the other parts of his personality lie dormant. Such a man approaches a woman with a strength and superiority that often attracts because it seems to be masculine strength. He has been brought up by a strict father and this has probably been followed up by going to a strict school. Later on he is hired by strict employers who often seek this kind of individual and so the pattern continues. Now such a man doesn't approach his mate with a very deep physical passion at all, but he does attract her by the self-assurance that comes from the identification with the tyrants of his youth. He talks, if you like, like a giant with authority. He talks as if he is quite assured. He has no doubts about anything; on almost any subject, he will appear to be informed. He gives the appearance of a gift of immense strength which appeals to some elements of the feminine spirit. An attachment is made and a courtship begins on that basis. But because he is dominated by this super-ego, this rigid conscience, his relationship can produce a sense of guilt. Ordinary sex relationships, however charmingly they are entered into, are clouded by a feeling of guilt. And even when these people are married, the same guilt in a less obvious form follows them as when they had pre-marital relations, because they have found themselves guilty for giving way to primitive desire. And their women are confused, because after having what appeared to be a joyous sexual embrace, they find their man moody and sometimes cruel because of his feeling of restlessness and guilt. Now in the face of such a peculiar character driven by his strict conscience, the woman, if she is not careful, can act in a way that destroys the real richness of her personality; and like the sleeping beauty, she never awakens out of her sleep of virginity for, instead of loving her mate in equality and fellowship, she submits to his rigidity and develops an over-feminine, masochistic type of temperament which almost seeks to be bullied. Some people live permanently in this sort of peculiar arrangement where the woman is over-feminine and the man is apparently masculine but in actual fact is domineering and rigid. When a man is like this, he is often very tight with money and damnably obstinate as well so that the wife has a hard time even getting the money from him to pay her bills.

The second kind of character-formation I want to talk about is that of a man who is dominated by his instinctual drives. This type is becoming more common and it is fashionable nowadays to profess this type of behaviour. And men doing so are under the impression that they are really getting to know their girls. In marriage or courtship with this type of man, the emphasis is on sensual expression. He will maintain that the pursuit of such sensual expression is a sign of freedom. Such people are potent and healthy because of a lack of repression. And the pill is available to prevent the possibility of children.

Now what happens in these cases is that although they think that the personality is free because they behave this way, instead of being free they are dominated by instinctual impulses in a manner which would place them millions of years back on the evolutionary scale. They don't represent the cultural level of our civilisation; they represent the cultural level of paleolithic man. And they are akin to the brute in this way, the brute who failed to evolve. For civilisation has been built on the correct channelling of these instincts, not on allowing the instincts to control behaviour. Now the young people today feel it is wonderful because they can have freedom of sex. And it is a wonderful and exciting experience to express instincts that have been subdued for years. And marriages based on these attitudes are often glorious marriages for a few years, for the emphasis is on the pure sensual delights of the body. But because they are based on the biological gifts of each other and not on the total personality of each other, they fail. A very beautiful girl can biologically attract scores of men to her by her beauty, and if allied to it is a free sensuality, then she is rapturously sought. But when her body starts to age, when the lines of her face start to set in, when the pain of living together and all its problems mark her countenance, when a certain stooping takes place through being wounded, as well as growing old, her biological lovers go looking for a new relationship; for they base a relationship not on the spirit of a girl but on her sensual attraction. And many beautiful women, after a few years of rapturous married life, are shattered by the infidelity of their men. For their men in their infidelity to them have been in a fidelity to their impulses, because their impulses respond as all other impulses do; they respond to the finest creatures they can get. This was the struggle in nature that Darwin talked about; the prettiest and finest animals attract the greatest number of lovers. And any number of men, who for quite a number of years enrich and give strength to a woman for this reason, can get up and walk out on her because they have got tired of her. Her sensuality bores, she is not as spontaneous as she used to be, she is not as vital as she used to be, she is tired, she is nursing children. And so the man finds another lover. And such women often have to endure the added shame of a husband's infidelity which is paraded quite openly. And the shattering effect of her husband's sensuality being transferred to another woman drives her to become once again a 'sleeping beauty.' Thus a sensual man can, for a number of years, apparently gratify everything a girl has but gratify nothing in the end because he has never loved her personality.

There is a third type of character formation which a man may have, where the 'ego' functions are dominant. This type tends to stress the intellectual aspects of life and very often he will embark on a sort of scholarly courtship with a woman. Their relationship can have a physical tinge and it can have acknowledged sensuality; but they are attracted to one another because they both love literature or they both love painting or music or university life. Many such couples are students and they love the involvement of student days. They are both thrilled with one another and they talk the most gorgeous talk with one another; other people bore them to tears. I've known courtships like these to end tragically. I can think of one young fellow who became a doctor and who was in love with a girl who had a mind like his own, a beautiful, exquisite mind. And apparently he courted her up to the very last minute when he went to Canada and left her completely alone. He was now in a new kind of life and this relationship no longer interested him. I was able to help the girl save her mind but I wasn't able to save her from years of heart-break, for she was quite sure that this man was her mate; even he had been quite sure. They used to have such enthralling discussions, but that's how it all ended!

Well, you may ask, what kind of a relationship can men and women have which isn't based on intellectuality, instinct or the super-ego?

The truth is that the only way to ever get into a true love relationship is to get in touch—not with the body, important as it is, and not with mind, important as it is, and not with the inter-relationship with authority and subservience—but with the ultimate spirit of the person. The only way for a man to get to know a woman is to get to know her ultimate spirit. The relationship is one of the uniqueness of the spirit, because there aren't two girls the same and there aren't two boys the same. Every girl is a sleeping beauty in her own right. Until a man discovers the essential uniqueness of a woman, her strength and tenacity and spiritual power, he will never know his woman. When he only attends to a beautiful, poetic expression, or to her intellectual accomplishments, or to the ravishing delights of her body, he doesn't know his woman at all. And I think that a man will feel he has got no authority to physically touch a woman until he has had some contact with her ultimate spirit and personality. You don't know your woman until she is at bay with you. And when you try to penetrate into the innermost mystery of a woman, determined you are going to get her, it is like a fellow walking along a plain of beautiful grass and flowers and suddenly coming up against a barrier of mighty mountains with their heads covered with snow, and full of precipitous pathways and dangers.

A woman will only really awaken when she is at spiritual bay with an intruder who is determined to investigate
those icy mountains. A woman must know that when it
comes to the crunch, a man is not faint-hearted. And this
is the excitement of getting to know the ultimate woman.
Even if she is the damnedest liar under the sun and spends
your money as if money grew in the garden and dresses
herself far too well for you to afford and all the rest of
it, then be quite sure it is only camouflage thrown in your
face—confetti—lest you approach and be blinded with
petals in your eye! But if you know anything about wom-
en you will know that her passionate sexuality cannot
be obtained by sensuality; sensuality cannot arouse
sexual passion in a woman. This is an odd thing, because I know the sensualist thinks he can; he thinks
he can arouse the sexual passion of a woman: but she
only gives mechanically and grudgingly. But in a lad
who will dare to invade the innermost recesses of her
and find out all that she is, she has got a most eager desire to disrobe. Even if before she has been quite staid
and superior, a self-defended fortress, she now has yearnings and hopes and palpitations. But woe to a chap who
is only a tin soldier, who goes on that journey, who is
only a Saturday afternoon, grab-a-cushion volunteer. God
help him! For this is not an adventure for the dilettante.
A woman is the one untamable thing in the universe and
is therefore very well worth finding, well worth knowing.

Now if you are going to have the kind of courtship I
am talking about, your total fundamental self must be involved. You have got to give a woman nothing less than
your own wild, audacious, determined spiritual self, and
stand where you think you should stand, and stand un-
breakably firm for what you believe to be true, even if
you are threatened with expulsion, even if you are ex-
pelled. For expulsion is only one of the threats a woman
may fling out when she is at bay. And the spirit of a
man who can withstand this barrage will be ultimately
strong and tender with a woman; he won't play with her
emotions. He will sense when she is suicidal and he won't
mock her. He will sense those queer moods which come

over women which they themselves can't understand; neither can other women understand them. It is only in the love of a mature man that women find something to counterpoise their nature, that they can have peace and security.

CIVILISATION

CHAPTER FIFTEEN

In the light of the previous chapters you can see how profound marriage is. It is not just a question of two people coming and trying to live together; it is two people coming together with various levels of disturbance in their personalities. And they have got to find some kind of compassion, some kind of light, some kind of love, that will help them to help each other through the crisis of development.

Now I'm not pessimistic about it, for I'm sure if we had a real understanding of marriage, we would realise perhaps that the true nature of marriage is altogether different from the sentimental conception of love which is based on romantic literature. We have discovered that the purpose of marriage is really to recreate each other, to heal and save each other, to transcend each other, to lift each other up to new heights, to purify each other and ultimately to weld together two souls in an indissoluble unity, the miraculous achievement of life where two really become one. And when two people become one, they *are* civilisation. Civilisation comes on earth when two people merge in this way because these two also bind together the generations that have gone before. Instead of pitching their old people out and forgetting them, they will

131

regard them as an essential part of the whole wonderful
pattern of the generations. And this is civilisation. Civilisation is the achievement of the control of the spirit of
man over the profound evolutionary forces that lie in the
depths of the unconscious. Man consciously represents
his present civilisation; but deep in his unconscious he
carries millions of years of evolution, millions of years
of earlier growth, and his chief function is the transmuta-
tion of all these forces. And the culmination of this comes
with a true marriage which brings about nothing less
than the building of a genuine, fundamental, trustworthy
civilisation, where people are interlocked by sincere love
and concern, where they bear with one another through
every vicissitude of life and draw little children unto
them with tenderness and pleasure and in their home
present to the surrounding neighbours a place of beauty
and refreshment to come to.

Within everyone there is a drive to be better and longing towards beauty and perfection. This light which is
within everyone is the lamp of evolution, or if you want
to speak of it in religious terms, the spirit of God in the
heart of man. If you follow this, you will be drawn out of
yourself, out of your selfishness, to love others. In the
marriage situation if you are drawn out of yourself towards your mate and she likewise, in this way you bring
about a mutual redemption. For in recognising and transcending your own unconscious drives you can see very
clearly that your little woman, for example, is tied in a
moody knot. She can't right herself; she's bogged down;
she needs someone to put his arms around her and say,
'Come home, darling, and don't worry; just be yourself
and I am with you.' Whether it is the man or the woman
who can do that, you will have followed the light; in religious language, you have brought the Kingdom of Heav-
en on earth. You have brought it into yourself first by
surrendering to it; and then you have drawn your wife
or your husband into it by its healing power. So marriage
offers a tremendous opportunity for the conquest of our
primitive drives. Marriage is a splendid institution in
evolution, a marvellous institution. It allows you to dwell

together for years, night and day; it allows you to meet each other in all the crises of emotion that come in any lively man or woman's life; it allows you to build on earth a foundation that will not perish and against which all the vicissitudes of life can beat in vain. Such a home will be founded in eternity, not in time, on truth, not on makebelieve, and unto such men and women comes a new excellence, an incarnation. For Christ did not want himself to be the only Word made Flesh; he called us all children of God! And so the mystery of the incarnation becomes known to us in our own experience, by transcending ourselves and knowing this tender, ever illuminating force growing within us. We learn to surrender the demands of selfishness to those of love. We follow the light within so that all self-centered desires fall away.

Now is it worthwhile? Is marriage a splendid opportunity? Is marriage a magnificent situation? Is marriage a place where we can prepare a new age for our children so that they may be born into a new excellence, a new atmosphere of beauty, where they can feel the quality of good immanent in our homes, where they are aware of mercy, of forgiveness and of the serenity that comes to those who make this effort? Isn't there every reason to have the courage to be married?